To,

Susannah

the very finest
of chef!

Bon appetit!

[signature]

KNEAD TO KNOW

KNEAD TO KNOW

A History of Baking

Neil Buttery

ICON

Published in the UK and USA in 2024 by
Icon Books Ltd, Omnibus Business Centre,
39–41 North Road, London N7 9DP
email: info@iconbooks.com
www.iconbooks.com

ISBN: 978-183773-121-3
eBook: 978-183773-122-0

Typeset by SJmagic DESIGN SERVICES, India.

Printed and bound in the UK.

CONTENTS

INTRODUCTION

This book is an exploration of baking and its associated terminology, techniques, science and innovation as well as its important place in culture, all viewed through the lens of history. Taking a historical perspective doesn't just give us an idea of what things were discovered when, it also gives us an idea of how our understanding of the science of baking has evolved. I could have chosen to write an encyclopaedia, but I believe the best way to understand most complex things is to see them evolve: the changes, the improvements, both expected and accidental. I hope, ultimately, that it will build upon your own understanding and intuition so that in the end you will be a better baker.

This brings me to the word *evolution*: when we think of such a phenomenon, we may think that every step is an improvement, an incremental elevation toward some peak of perfection. This is not always the case. Sometimes things have to become simpler, sometimes knowledge is lost, and skills are forgotten. It depends upon your perspective too, of course: are affordable factory-produced cakes, made of processed ingredients, with their indefinite shelf lives an improvement on a wonky homemade cake or not? The answer depends upon whether you are asking Mary Berry or Mr Kipling.

Names evolve and change as new foods are invented, but sometimes names *don't* change as foods veer greatly from their previous forms, causing confusion. For example, if I ask you to imagine a cake, what immediately springs to mind? A nice cream cake, perhaps? A Mississippi mud pie? Or did you think of a fairy cake, or a Scottish oatcake? A Jaffa Cake? A bread cake? Tracing the history of these things helps us explain the similarities and the differences, the steps forwards and the steps back.

Much of this book draws on my own research, writing and cooking. I started writing my blog, *Neil Cooks Grigson*, where I cooked every recipe in Jane Grigson's *English Food*, in 2007 as a hobby. I then moved to America in 2010 for my work as a scientist. There I continued cooking Jane's recipes but also started a second (and much more popular!) blog, *British Food: a History* in 2011, so obsessed had I become with food history and traditions. My American friends enjoyed trying all the strange, foreign British food I was cooking, and without realising it, I had built quite a repertoire of skills and recipes. In 2012 I resigned from my job, moved back to Britain and started up my own artisan food stall. I had no special equipment beyond a food mixer, some baking trays, scone cutters and some pie tins. The market became a pop-up restaurant, became a bricks-and-mortar restaurant. The restaurant closed in late 2017 and since then I have concentrated more on research and writing about food and social history.

Baking has been a focus throughout my rather meandering career: baked goods are (as you will soon see) some of the most simple and complex of foodstuffs. They require skill and judgement to make, and they are beloved by all: you'd be hard pushed to find someone willing to turn down a delicious pie or baked pudding. Most importantly, many recipes require very little special equipment or paraphernalia to make.

Knead to Know is not a recipe book, but you will find recipes for many of the delicious baked goods mentioned in this book on my blogs – and many more that are not. At this point I must make clear my other inspirations, because they are the sources I have used to write this book. There are centuries of excellent cookery writing from individuals such as Robert May, Hannah Glasse, Elizabeth Raffald, Eliza Acton and Charles Elmé Francatelli to name but a few. I hope that, after reading this book, you hunt out their books and cook their recipes; in the main, their works are available online to download for free. There is also the great work of other food historians and writers like Alan Davidson, Ivan Day, Annie Gray, Peter Brears, Harold McGee, Regula Ysewijn, Sam Bilton, Laura Mason, Marc Meltonville, Glyn Hughes and Elizabeth David. All of my sources are given in the bibliography at the back of this book.

Tracking the evolution of anything complex inevitably results in the growth of evolutionary trees, with many branches diverging from major limbs to form new groups. As an animal that likes to compartmentalise, humans don't like it when some things have a foot in more than one camp or when there are grey areas. Just when does pastry become biscuit, bread become cake? For this book to make sense I have had to split it into chapters, and you might not agree with the exact places I have drawn my lines, but we have to start somewhere. To that end, I have split the messy world of baking into the following subjects: griddlecakes and pancakes, bread, scones and cakes, pies and puddings, and patisserie. Each chapter is split into a series of short pieces, connected with the loose narrative of history in a way that is intuitive to me, and I hope will be to you. Each piece stands alone, so you can dip in and out, or read it from cover to cover, it's entirely up to you.

Now you know my approach, let's open our first can of worms with this question: What is baking?

It seems like an easy question to answer, doesn't it? In modern parlance, it's anything cooked in an oven, and I am sure there are many foods we will agree are baked: pound cakes, brandy snaps, gingerbread, meat pies, pasties, crumbles, macarons. But then there are other things that are baked in ovens but are not found in a bakery or on *The Great British Bake Off*; our Sunday 'roast' joint is actually baked, yet it is very obvious (I hope) that roast beef shouldn't be included in this book. Then there is a long list of foods that are not baked in ovens but would be remiss of me to miss out. I'm talking about crumpets, muffins, drop scones, pancakes, oatcakes and the like. As it happens, all of these foods are cooked upon a *bake*stone, directly over a fire, the invention of which precedes the oven by centuries. I am confident that you would agree with me that they should be included.

Then there is the most British of foods, the pudding. I am not suggesting for a second that black pudding should be included in the club; that would be ridiculous. But baked puddings like sticky toffee or Bakewell pudding have to be in there. And what about the hundreds of boiled and steamed puddings like Christmas, treacle and jam roly-poly pudding? And let's not forget their fried cousins: jam doughnuts and yum-yums. There's ice cream, jellies and all sorts of foods that might be included too. These are not baked but we think of them as all within the same realm. That said, I have largely chosen not to include these foods, simply to help narrow things down a bit; and so, all of the foods described in this book are baked either in an oven or on a griddle. Those are my rules, I just wonder how well I will stick to them.

GRIDDLECAKES
AND PANCAKES

I have laid out what I have and have not counted as baking in the introduction, so now we can begin our origin story properly, and ask ourselves: 'What was the first thing to be baked, and how was it achieved?' I hope I am on fairly solid ground when I say that the stuff – the raw ingredients, as it were – must have been some flour mixture of one or more grains: wheat or barley most likely. Grains had been toasted and cooked in pots of water before someone had the idea of grinding them up first, this we know. Grinding is a natural progression from roasting; if you have ever toasted your own grains or whole spices, you will know just how brittle and easy to break they are, and just how delicious they taste when broken. Combining cooking with grinding was an extremely important notion: cooking breaks down a food and liberates nutrients, making it easier to chew and digest; in science-parlance, the food is more 'nutritionally available'. Grinding or crushing is like pre-chewing, making the food quicker to cook and easier to ingest. When mixed with water, the starch and gluten inside a cereal grain can mix to form simple batters. These batters could be made into porridges or gruels, or the basis of soups, but how were they baked? It has been long established that from some time in the Mesolithic Age (10,000 to 8,000 BCE) fires were built inside rings of stones, which eventually became hot. However, archaeological evidence from the Black Desert, Jordan, in 2018, moved the date back 2,000 years. Remnants of flatbreads cooked by a hunter-gatherer society on flat stones were unearthed and analysed and were found to contain wild wheat and barley and mashed roots.

Stone is a poor conductor of heat, but once it is hot, it remains hot for a long time, and a blob of dough or a thick batter will cook very well on a flat stone. After this discovery – perhaps by accident – flatter stones were chosen and they were worked to be smoother. The first bakestones were made, and humans got their first taste of hearthcakes, the origin of all baked goods.

Processing and cooking carbohydrate, protein and nutrient-rich wholegrains changed the course of human history: nomadic tribes settled in a single spot in order to grow more of these cereals. The hunter-gatherer had become a farmer and from this point, villages, then towns and cities – *civilisations* – would form. This meant humans would become more and more dependent upon these grains and better at cooking with them. They also became better at processing and refining them, and at the same time were able to select the plants with the highest yields, domesticating them. Grinding and cooking them maximised the nutrition inside those plants. This could be achieved by making gruels of course, but with baking, you get something extra: toasty crusts, soft and fluffy interiors.

Archaeological digs at and around Stonehenge have revealed that the people who lived and probably celebrated or worshipped here certainly ground wheat, grew a lot of hazelnuts and spent a great deal of time searching for honey. Simple cakes made with ground wheat, ground hazelnuts, honey and probably a little water have been cooked up on hearthstones and found to be not only very 'nutritionally available' but also very *delicious*.

FIRST GRAINS

In recent decades the variety of foods we consume has gone through somewhat of a bottleneck, and this is certainly true for the different types of grains, and flours made from them. There was a time when most British communities grew several different cereals, the precise proportion of wheat, barley, oats and rye dependent upon locale. Cereals were first domesticated in a bow-shaped strip of land sitting across what is today the Middle East, somewhere around the eighth and seventh century BCE. This large strip is known as the Fertile Crescent. Here barley and wheat (and pease*) were the first to be grown, with rye and oats coming later. Two key changes also occurred in the farming and selection of barley and wheat. On the stalk of cereals, each grain is covered by an outer husk which must be removed (*shilled*); these skilled farmers managed to produce

---

* This is the old name for peas, and it was both the singular and plural. Pease was also for baking the much-hated peasebread.

strains that were 'naked', i.e. had a husk that easily shilled itself before harvest time. Second, the 'ears' of corn and barley were bred to cling more tightly to their stalks and not blow away in the wind as the wild types do; grasses disperse their seeds via wind, so it's an adaptation they have naturally, one that humans have managed to undo.

Let's have a look at the four main cereal crops in turn:

1. **Barley** spread like wildfire out of the Fertile Crescent through communities and countries because of its hardiness and ability to adapt to novel environments, and it has been successfully grown from the Artic Circle to the tropics. It has been ground into flour and made into a variety of cakes and breads in Ancient Babylonia, Egypt, India and the Mediterranean. It was the bread of choice in ancient Rome until it was superseded by wheat. Barley breads and griddlecakes were commonly eaten throughout Britain before the twentieth century, though these days it is grown mainly for the beer and whisk(e)y industries.

2. **Rye** was originally considered a weed and it followed wherever barley and wheat led, much to the annoyance of farmers. It was only domesticated around 1000 BCE when it was realised that it grew well in poor soils and cold climates, and because of this it became a key crop across northern Europe. Rye was grown across Britain from the early medieval period, though more for its stalks than its grain, because they made for excellent thatching for roofs. Rye is the traditional flour in French *pain d'épices* and Germanic *pumpernickel*. Its short-stranded gluten molecules

make it suitable for griddlecakes and pancakes. Rye was so popular in Germany that wheat production only overtook it in 1957.

3. **Oats** were the last of the true cereals to be domesticated, and were, like rye, considered a weed, but their ability to thrive in cold, wet environments made oats a favoured crop in Northern England, Northern Wales, Scotland and Ireland and – again, like rye – was cultivated from the early medieval period. A great variety of griddlecakes emerged from these regions as a result.

4. **Wheat** is considered the king of cereals – at least in the Western world – and this is because of its gluten: not only does it contain a large amount of it, but the gluten chains are longer than other cereals', making griddlecakes and bread more bouncy and doughs easier to handle. Its cultivation was comparatively low across medieval Europe because it was difficult to grow in wet conditions. This made wheat rare and therefore gave it status.

The first wheat to be domesticated was called einkorn. It has two sets of chromosomes (this is the DNA we receive from our parents, one set from mum and one from dad), which makes it a diploid ('two-sets') organism.* At some point, it hybridised with a wild goosegrass to produce a new species. Hybridisation is common in plants and means that the plant then receives sets of chromosomes from two species, producing a hybrid with four

---

* Einkorn was thought to have gone extinct until a small population of it was discovered in the 1970s, where it was being cultivated in a small community in the Vacheuse region of France. It was being used to make a local porridge.

sets of chromosomes (a tetraploid). From these plants, emmer and durum wheat were created. The former preferred arid conditions and was taken to Africa, while the latter was used in Europe for pasta. Then the tetraploid domesticated wheat hybridised again with another species of goosegrass, producing a variety of wheat with six sets of chromosomes (it was now hexaploid). From this new form of wheat, spelt was derived, and all modern wheats are derived from this hexaploid ancestor. Why? The hybridisation is key: there was a huge amount of genetic variation trapped inside, so many different strains could be created. Today 30,000 varieties of wheat are actively grown. Of all wheat grown around the world, 90 per cent of it is hexaploid, and coming in second place, just a smidge under 5 per cent, is tetraploid durum for pasta.

HEARTHSTONES, BAKESTONES AND GRIDDLES

Cooking on a flat piece of stone, as opposed to cooking in a pot, meant that instead of having a liquid gruel or thick porridge, you had a solid cake cooked on a hearthstone that was portable, could be eaten with fingers, passed around and wrapped around other foods. It could soak up the juices from meat, it was brown and toasty. Hearthstone cooking was, simply, more versatile and more delicious, and the products from the bakestone have been enjoyed for millennia. One of the reasons foods cooked on bakestones or griddles have endured is simplicity: a flat, hot surface can be made by just sweeping ash away from a hearth and cooking some dough straight on it. Eventually folk started to make bakestones (or *bakstones* in Northern England and Scotland) from 'thin slabs of any locally available stone which could withstand the heat of the fire'.[1] However, from the Elizabethan Age, most common were the cast-iron griddles (or *girdles* in Northern England and Scotland). Curiously, in some regions, they retained the name of bak(e)stone, despite the fact that the material they were made from had changed. The great benefit of iron is that it can be fashioned into a variety of shapes. The standard shape, however, quickly became a round disc with a large, curved handle reaching right over it, perpendicular to the base: this meant that you could move it without burning yourself and that you could hang it over a fire.

Bakestones and griddles are still used today, but they have been taken over by other, perhaps more versatile implements like cast iron skillets. In the UK the making of a good griddlecake or pancake is a skill on the wane – aside from the annual Pancake Day crêpe, how often do we cook some of these up? It seems almost inconceivable that we might knock up a batch of muffins at home. Griddlecakes and pancakes were once the backbone of the country, especially for the working classes; ovens were expensive pieces of kit, and their social rank may not have allowed them to have one installed. Even then, they were only really good for baking large fluffy bloomers of wheaten bread, an expensive cereal compared to the other ones: 'one of the great points about … all of the tribe of griddlecakes,' wrote Elizabeth David, 'was that they provided a means of using meals and flours such as barley, buckwheat, oatmeal, which are not suitable for bread proper.'[2] Indeed: low or no gluten-containing flours, if forced into the shape of a large bloomer, would come out of the oven as flat as, well, a pancake. You could have had your loaves baked in a public bakery, but even the more populous towns of Britain didn't have one: Manchester was without one until well into the nineteenth century. This meant that, for a large proportion of the country, griddlecakes and pancakes were the only way of making baked goods at home and were a key element of the community. Scots *baxter* (baker) women would bake oatcakes on their hearths for those who worked too many hours to bake them themselves.

There are some rules of thumb when it comes to using bakestones and griddles: they are tricky to use at first, and being made with stoneware or cast iron, they take a while to heat up, and a while to cool down. Scottish food historian F. Marian McNeill helps us out with some tips in her classic book *The Scots Kitchen* (first published 1929, second edition 1968). To test the heat, sprinkle it with flour: if it takes a few seconds to brown, you are good to go. She also tells us that 'the girdle is floured for dough and greased for batter'. She emphasises that 'only the best materials should be used', and that dough should be handled as little as possible and 'turned only once'.[3] Every stage is important: sifting the flour twice, mixing it correctly and methodically, and – of course – the ingredients must be of excellent quality. As with all 'simple' foods, attention to detail is of paramount importance.

They may not be the backbone of the country anymore, but those that have hung on are loved dearly today: Scottish, Derbyshire and Staffordshire oatcakes, wheaten farls, potato cakes, pikelets, crumpets, muffins, drop scones, bannocks, Welsh cakes, crempog las, crêpes. And then let's not forget those that have been welcomed into our food culture from other countries: chapatis, tortillas, blinis, fluffy American pancakes. What variety! Our lives would certainly be less delicious without them, that's for sure.

GRINDING GRAINS

In order for us to bake, our ancestors needed to grind their grains into meal, and up until the last 100 years or so, this was achieved by grinding them between stones. When we think of stoneground flour today, we perhaps imagine gently turning windmill sails on balmy autumn days, and we think of the flour produced as wholesome, the real deal.

The first evidence of humans using grinding stones goes back to Southern France, 10,000 BCE, where simple pestles and mortars have been discovered that were used to grind pigments, but we can assume too that similar instruments were used to grind other things such as grains. It wouldn't have made a fine flour, more a crushed grain for gruels and porridges. The next step in the evolution of the mill is the saddle quern. It is an adapted pestle and mortar made especially for grinding grains, made up of a large, flat stone, with a depression in the middle that slopes down on two opposite sides – the saddle. Grain was strewn on it and was crushed by scraping a large stone rolling pin which was thicker in the middle over it. It was very hard work and was usually done by women. They have been depicted on Egyptian friezes, but they travelled and became popular as far away as neolithic Ireland. This quern spread throughout Europe and was used in many private dwellings in Britain.

Flour, as we think of it today, was first made using the man-powered rotary 'hourglass' quern, the origins of which remain obscure, but they were certainly being used in ancient Egypt. It was made up of a fixed, flat, round lower stone, with a second stacked on top, stabilised with an axle. Wooden arms protruded horizontally so that it could be turned (usually by slaves). The stones had grooved channels carved into them, down which good-quality fine flour cascaded. This was very efficient compared to the earlier types of quern, but it was limited by the strength of one's own workforce. The next major change happened in the second century, when waterpower was harnessed to turn the top stone. These watermills were installed all over the Roman Empire, including England. The Romans left, but their mills remained part of early medieval life: there are 6,000 watermills listed in *Domesday Book*. The earliest found in the British Isles is in Tamworth and dates from the seventh century. The windmill was invented in Persia around 1000 CE. As trade and people moved westwards, so did ideas and technology, and in the case of the windmill it travelled to Britain via Holland and the Low Countries.

These water- and windmills used large stones, up to 1.5 meters in diameter and very heavy. The stones would often wear and chip, meaning that one's flour came full of grit. Folk didn't want to accidentally chip a tooth when eating their bread, so to avoid this, they sifted, or 'bolted', it. But this process of bolting also removed a great deal of the bran, so a softer, whiter flour was made. Bolting has been done by the Ancient Egyptians, so whiteness appears to be an ancient desire, not just a modern one.

In medieval Britain, where the majority lived under the thumb of a feudal lord, people had their access to flour highly controlled, and were forced to have their grain milled in a communal mill owned by the lord of the manor. The miller was usually employed by the lord, and for each sack of flour produced, they both took a cut. In many villages, the smaller home querns were banned, making it illegal to grind one's own flour. It was also a pain to transport their grain across the village. Consequently, the village miller was usually intensely disliked by the community, and he certainly wasn't the friendly, well-loved Windy Miller we might imagine him to be.

With the dismantling of the feudal system* and then the agricultural revolution of the eighteenth century and the industrial revolution of the nineteenth century, millstones were turned under the power of steam, and for the first time industrial quantities of flour were produced. Now, the limiting factor in flour production was the production of grain itself.

---

* This took longer than you might think, hanging on to the early nineteenth century in some places in the British Isles.

ANATOMY OF A GRAIN

It's time for a brief biology lesson. There has been, and there will be much more, talk of starch, gluten, germ and bran. Let's take a small sidestep and look at where all of these things lie within a grain of wheat. A grain is technically a fruit, not in the sense that an apple or a mango is a fruit, but in the botanical sense, because a fruit contains the germ, or embryo, of a plant as well as the nutrients to help that germ develop into a seedling. This may or may not be wrapped in a delicious layer of flesh; in the case of cereals, it is not. The nutritional part of the grain is called the endosperm and it is an elongated oval shape. It makes up the bulk of the grain, around 85 per cent. It is made almost entirely of carbohydrate and protein, and a great deal of that protein, especially in wheat cultivars, is gluten. The endosperm is wrapped in a thin casing just a few cells thick called the aleurone layer. It makes up a small proportion of the whole grain; however, writes Harold McGee, it 'contain[s] oil, minerals, protein, vitamins, enzymes, and flavour out of proportion to its size'.

Stuck to the bottom of the endosperm is the germ, or embryo. It is very small, making up just 2 per cent of the whole grain, and is difficult to see when looking at a grain of wheat. However, the embryo of a peanut is very easy to spot; when the peanut is split in two, it sits nestled on the inside of the blunt end of one half of the nut. Like the aleurone layer, the embryo is small but packed with nutrients.

The endosperm and embryo are wrapped up in several protective seed coats. This is the bran, and it makes up around

15 per cent of the whole grain. Indeed, what I have described *is* the whole grain: bran, germ and endosperm. White flours have the germ, bran and aleurone layer sifted out, leaving behind the starch and protein-rich endosperm. After sifting, the nutritional profile of the flour changes greatly. White flour contains 62 per cent less vitamin K and 48 per cent less folic acid, but contains 11 per cent more calories and 15 per cent more carbohydrate compared to whole wheat flour.[4] A great deal of the grain's flavour and character is also lost. However, by sifting out the nutrients, the shelf life of the white flour is markedly increased, and – of course – we get to enjoy more tender, more pillowy, bouncy bakes: something we, as a species, seem to prize over everything else, including flavour.

THE OATCAKES OF BRITAIN

'Oats: A grain, which in England is generally given to horses, but in Scotland supports the people.' Samuel Johnson[5]

There once was a great diversity of oatcakes in Britain, and despite Dr Samuel Johnson's thoughts on them, they were eaten not just across Scotland but also the North of England and the Midlands, and they were dearly loved. I say *were* because they are almost extinct in England now. In the 'eighteenth century, sacks of oatmeal were as common a sight in Manchester Market as sacks of wheat were in the South', wrote food writer Jane Grigson, who was originally from Northumberland.[6] They do live on in Derbyshire and Staffordshire – but they are just about hanging on. These oatcakes are soft and thick, like a dense and very oaty drop scone, and are cooked on a griddle or bakestone. Today they are made with fine oatmeal and wheat flour (the latter making them easier to roll or fold), water, salt and baking powder; but they were once made from oatmeal (a mix of coarse and finely ground was the best), salt and water, the mixture made a day or two before they were to be cooked so the batter could sour and become naturally leavened by wild yeasts; a rare example of a traditional sourdough in English cookery. Leavening is the process of introducing air bubbles to a dough, making it rise and bake more tenderly. Today batters are leavened by the chemical action of baking powder and sadly lack the sour flavour that was once relished.

Oatcakes were made in Yorkshire too, well into the twentieth century, but all are now extinct and just a few folk remember eating them. They were commonly made in great numbers by housewives. A sourdough batter was made from oatmeal, salt and water, ladlefuls of it flung at an angle onto a hot griddle so the batter spread out into a long oval streak, before being removed and dried out in front of the fire. They were fiendishly difficult to make. Another, called riddlebread, was made by pouring the batter onto an oatmeal-strewn board (called a riddle board) and was deftly slid onto a slightly greased griddle. Yet another was made by scraping a pool of batter across the bakestone. Sadly, all of these skills are now gone.*

---

* Only one person that I know of has been able to work out how those Yorkshire housewives did it: food historian Ivan Day.

Scottish oatcakes, however, are extremely popular, not just in Scotland but across the whole of the British Isles. They are not made from a batter; instead a dough made up of oatmeal, salt, water, bicarbonate of soda, and a tiny amount of fat is rolled out, cut into circles and cooked on the griddle. Traditionally made ones curl up attractively around the edges. They became a staple food in Scotland in the seventeenth century when oats displaced barley as the main cereal crop. When baked they were treated as bread: eaten with butter and marmalade for breakfast, with soups, and – just like today – with cheese.

If we love Scottish oatcakes so much why have the others disappeared? Perhaps it was to do with the changing family structures from the latter half of the twentieth century, when fewer women were full-time housewives, and because they required both time and practised skill to make, they simply vanished. Scottish oatcakes, meanwhile, could be easily baked in ovens, lending them well to commercial production (though, sadly, their edges no longer curl up). Historians Laura Mason and Catherine Brown may have pinned down the real reason: the English and their culture of aspiration meant that oatcakes lost out to white bread, while in Scotland – where wheaten bread was certainly available – it remained, because of their 'greater understanding of the nutritional value of oatmeal'.[7] And they were right, because up until recently, the oats grown in Scotland were much more nutritious than any of the wheat that was grown not just in Scotland, but across the whole of the British Isles.

29

WHY SO TASTY?

As soon as humans developed bakestone technology, a great diversity of pancakes and griddlecakes were conjured up, but what was the attraction in the first place? Cooking starchy foods makes them more digestible, especially when that food has been ground into meal and mixed with water. This happens via the process of gelatinisation, and to understand this we need to know a little about the microscopic constituents of cells called starch grains. They are roughly spherical in shape and are made up of layers and layers of starch molecules. These grains are too small to be ground by millstones and remain intact. When flour and water are mixed to form a simple batter, some water is absorbed into the grains, causing them to swell. When they are heated, enough water is absorbed into the starch grains to disrupt the layers of starch, which begin to slough away from the grain surface. Starch molecules are made up of long chains of glucose molecules, and as these polymers disperse into the water they tangle and weave, capturing some of the water and forming a gel, thus thickening the mixture. This is gelatinisation. The benefit to whoever eats a griddlecake is that the cooked starch is easier, quicker and more efficient to digest than raw. This is because gelatinised starch is nicely spread out and not fixed inside starch grains, meaning that the enzyme that digests starch into glucose within our bodies, amylase, can get to work immediately, acting before the food is even swallowed. If you were to eat some pure starch, such as cornflour, cooked in water, there would be a spike in your blood sugar levels that is very similar compared to if you had eaten pure glucose. If you ate raw cornflour and water, the peak is only a third of the size compared to the cooked starch.

But there is more to baked foods than this, and that is the glorious, delicious golden-brown coating which develops upon its surface as it cooks. It is something so inviting, for we know that within this delicious-smelling and tasting exterior is a nutrient-rich, easily digestible interior. Scores of aromatic compounds are created when baked goods brown, and it is achieved by the processes of caramelisation and Maillard reactions. Caramelisation occurs when sugars are heated and begin to react to produce chemicals that smell and taste both sweet and complex: caramel, butterscotch, vanilla, hazelnut and even fruity-smelling and tasting molecules are produced. When sugar gets very hot and the coating is very dark, bitter chemicals begin to form.

The Maillard reactions are more complex. It is the reaction between sugars and amino acids, the building blocks of proteins. The reaction was first described by the French chemist Louis C. Maillard in the 1910s. A huge array of compounds can be produced as a result of the reaction, providing savoury, earthy, mushroom, vegetal, meaty and even chocolatey or floral aromas. Curiously, this controlled burning of our food makes the outside less digestible, but because it's just a thin layer it doesn't matter, and we have evolved to associate an inside that is tender and easy to digest with the complex, nutrition-less, but very tasty, products of baking on the outside. Some of these chemicals may even be carcinogenic; don't worry, though, we have developed a resistance to these more sinister products, a testament to the importance eating baked foods has had in the evolutionary history of the human species.

PAST PANCAKES

'Abroad pancakes are usually open and piled up together. In England our pancakes are symbols of our insular detachment for each is rolled up by itself, aloof, with its own slice of lemon.' Dorothy Hartley, Food in England[8]

How does a pancake differ from a griddlecake? Well, food historian Alan Davidson believes them to be more tender, more rich, thinner and sweeter than your traditional griddlecake. He is of the opinion that the first pancakes are mentioned in the fourth-century Roman manuscript *Apicius*, and were made with flour, whisked eggs and milk, and served with honey and black pepper. Thin pancakes can be difficult to flip, and cooking them in a more mobile, lighter pan helps; after all, the clue is in their name.

In the United Kingdom, what image is conjured up when we think of pancakes? I reckon the vast majority of us think of a thin crêpe, the recipe being very similar to those of ancient Rome. Bubbles of gas and fats are usually added to make pancakes tender, but in the case of the crêpe, a different strategy is used to keep gluten and starch molecules from tangling together, and that is to space them out with plenty of liquid, therefore for good crêpe-like pancakes there must be a low ratio of flour compared to the other ingredients.

In the past our crêpe recipes were much more rich and indulgent, and were very tender indeed; a recipe from the eighteenth century called 'A Quire of Paper' instructs us to mix 125 grams of melted butter, 300 millilitres of cream, one egg, three tablespoons of sherry and one teaspoon of rose water with just 90 grams of flour (approximately three rounded tablespoons).[9] The name gives away how these pancakes are served – and certainly goes against Dorothy Hartley's opinion that they were always rolled up – for a quire of paper is a stack of 24 sheets of paper that have been folded over; so, in other words, a stack. I have made these pancakes a few times, and they are delicious, and so rich they eat like a dessert. They are extremely difficult to turn over without them breaking apart: a confident, deft flip is the only way to do it.

Britain has gone through a great bottleneck with regard to its diversity of pancakes, there was once a great variety and a great love of them – they certainly were not reserved only for Shrove Tuesday. England has been hit hardest, though Wales, Scotland and Ireland have managed to hold on to many of their traditions. In England we have said goodbye to delicious grainy Gloucester pancakes, their unique texture coming from the suet, not butter, used to enrich them. Singin' hinnies, described by Jane Grigson as 'the best of all griddlecakes', were eaten by all classes of people in Northwest England as recently as the last century. Just holding on for dear life are the large, floppy Derbyshire oatcakes, enjoyed dearly, but rarely travelling out of their county.

Ireland still has its farls, its boxty (potato pancakes), the Welsh have their crempog las (savoury crêpes flavoured with onions and parsley) and the frilly-edged light cakes made tart by the addition of sour cream. In Scotland there are bannocks, fermented sour scones and drop scones. The latter are the original fluffy pancakes, leavened chemically and served in stacks, pats of butter between each layer. These pancakes moved to Wales when Scottish miners and their families migrated there to work in the tin mines. Most significantly they also traversed the Atlantic to North America, where they were quickly assimilated into the culture to become the cornerstone of the American breakfast.

We need to remember there is more to pancakes than the annual crêpes, lemon juice and sugar on Shrove Tuesday: there are dozens of simple, delicious and comforting pancakes – and griddlecakes – to discover, and we have lost too many.

POSH PANCAKES

We think of pancakes as a fairly humble dish today, a great leveller. They might be eaten in all walks of life, but those who can afford luxury ingredients do so, especially if the food is being eaten in public. Two perfect examples of this are *crêpes Suzette* and the blini.

Crêpes Suzette is viewed these days perhaps as a slightly naff retro dish, but for 'the first two thirds of the 20th century was the epitome of luxury desserts'.[10] It is comprised of crêpes made with a batter enriched with tangerine juice and zest and three liqueurs: Curaçao, Maraschino and Kirsch. The delicate crêpes are fried in butter and stacked before a butter flavoured with the same aromatics as the batter is melted under a very low heat. One by one the pancakes are reintroduced to the pan, coated in the slowly melting butter and folded into quarters. Pancakes are added until most of the sauce is coating them. Quite the rich dish. And if that's not enough, the whole thing is doused in the three liqueurs and flambéed. Chef, restaurateur and raconteur Henri Charpentier* claimed to have invented the dish by accident while preparing a dessert for King Edward VII (then the Prince of Wales); Henri knocked over the three liqueurs and found the combination delicious. He doused crêpes in them, and the rest is history. They were a marvellous success and were named there and then in honour of the prince's female chaperone. Some advice at his point: always judge any food origin story where the creation of it was apparently accidental with great caution. They are almost always too good to be true. Charpentier did not invent this dish. The closest we can get to its beginnings is the recipe for it in Charles Escoffier's 1896 book *Le Guide Culinaire*. Traditionally all of the cooking was done at the diners' table in a fancy restaurant, therefore it came with a fancy price tag. 'A bit flashy', reckoned food writer

---

* Henri was, among many other things, the personal chef to the Rockefellers of New York. He lived quite the life.

Jane Grigson, 'and you pay far too much for the spectacle. Such a simple dish is best made at home.'[11]

The Russian buckwheat pancake blini is maybe where we go peak posh, because these small, gluten-free pancakes are often served with sour cream and beluga caviar. It wasn't always this way, but they have always been pretty rich. Their origin is lost to the mists of time, but they go back at least to the Middle Ages. Traditional recipes insist that the pancake is leavened by yeast, but because buckwheat flour has no gluten, extra air is introduced by adding whipped egg whites and cream. In pre-revolutionary Russia they were served in its equivalent of Mardi Gras, Maslenitsa, a week-long festival just before Lent. These pancakes were made to use up the animal products before the 40-day fast. Maslenitsa means literally 'butter week', and the blini, traditionally around ten centimetres in diameter, were fried in butter, then smothered in more butter and topped with preserved fish* and chopped boiled eggs, all washed down with glasses of vodka. Sounds pretty good to me.

Festival balls were held by the more well-to-do, and here the blini began to shrink in size; 'according to one theory', wrote *New York Times* journalist Sharon Lerch, 'their size had partly been a function of their wealth: The greater the quantity and expense of the various smoked, salted, and preserved fish, the smaller the blini.'[12] The people of Kyiv, being adjacent to the Black Sea, had greater access to sturgeon, and it was they who were first to top blini with a good dollop of caviar.

---

* Lent was particularly difficult in Russia at this time because not only were mammals and birds, and products thereof, disallowed, but also fish. Hard times.

WAFERS AND WAFFLES

These two beloved bakes are an offshoot of the griddlecakes tribe in that they are cooked between two hinged, patterned irons. Their common ancestor is something that resembles a wafer. It came from Ancient Greece, where *obelios* – flat crisp cakes – were cooked between two metal plates. They certainly caught on, and these crisp cakes would become one of the most popular foods of medieval Europe. They arrived in Britain via the Normans in the thirteenth century (the word *wāfre* being an Anglo-Norman one). They were a popular street food, and the snack of choice at any special events where waferers descended in such large numbers they were a fire hazard until a decree was issued that forced them to keep a minimum distance between each other.

The batter was a simple one: a mix of white flour, egg white,* ginger and – if swish – some sugar. The irons, which always had a pattern carved into them, were heated in a fire, removed, opened, and a small ladleful of the batter was poured upon one of them, before they were snapped shut. The irons would be so hot and create such pressure that 'the batter expanded rapidly, sending spurts of surplus mixture and jets of steam from their perimeter.'[13] They were eaten immediately while still crisp and hot.

---

* It is rare to find egg white in medieval and early modern recipes, as it was largely believed it was bad for one's constitution. The wafer seems to have been let off in this regard – and for good reason, because without egg white, the crisp texture typical of a wafer cannot be achieved.

Wafers were eaten in all walks of life and waferers were often hired for special events held by the gentry, clergy and royalty. Wafers crop up in *The Forme of Cury*, the first cookbook written in the English language, dating to around 1380. They are sprinkled with a sweet spice mixture (*powder douce*), cut into diamond shapes and served with broth. In 1486, the first Tudor king, Henry VII, was once showered with wafers cut into snowflake shapes on a visit to York. Most commonly, though, they were served toward the end of a feast with the other favourite of the day, the spiced, sweet wine known as hippocras. Ever since they have been associated with sweet foods in general, most famously as a crisp contrast to cold, creamy ice cream. Because it could be shaped easily and could be kept crisp if stored in air-tight boxes, the wafer became one of the first baked goods to be made in factories.

Waffles evolved from wafers inside continental Europe. They differ from wafers by being much thicker, resulting in a soft interior as well as a deliciously crisp exterior. They became particularly loved in the Low Countries where they were also sold as street food slathered in chocolate sauce and served with cream or ice cream. Waffles continued their popularity in North America when they were taken there by colonists in the seventeenth century. The ingredients were expensive, so they were only cooked up for special occasions like feasts and parties. They only became very popular with all classes after the 1964 New York World's Fair where they were made with the now characteristic honeycomb patterned plates and an extra-fluffy yeasted batter.* In America they are now a firm favourite at breakfast, and the requisite offering on even the most basic motels' breakfast menu. The deep honeycombs fill up lavishly with melted butter and maple syrup. In the Southern States, folk went a stage further and added fried chicken. Don't knock it till you've tried it.

KING ALFRED BURNS THE CAKES

The story is familiar to many of us: Alfred the Great, the late-eighth-century Anglo-Saxon king, exhausted and lost after beating the Danes in a vicious pitched battle, stumbles upon a herdsman's hut. The housewife within invites him in assuming him a mere soldier. She kindly offers him rest and nourishment as she has just put some cakes in the embers of her fire to bake. The cakes, no more than pieces of dough or paste, were so primitive they didn't even require a bakestone. She pops out to collect firewood, instructing her guest to keep an eye on the cakes lest they burn, but almost as soon as she leaves, knackered Alfred falls asleep. Upon her return, she is greeted by the smell of burning cakes and a sleeping soldier: 'What sort of careless man are you, who neglects to attend to burning bread? Never have I seen so negligent a man – one who doesn't even know how to turn ash-baked bread – and

---

* Other countries have different preferred patterns: Italian waffles have a pretty floral design, and Chinese ones are pressed into the shape of bubble wrap.

yet when it is put in front of you, you'll no doubt rush to eat it!' That's him told.

But what were these cakes, and how were they made? From the Middle Ages right up to the nineteenth and twentieth centuries, a home-baked loaf of bread was out of reach for the vast majority of households, which lacked a suitable oven and so relied on the oven (and skills) of local bakers, if there was one. For improvised baking in the medieval age, it was much easier to cook cakes directly over the fire. Cast iron equipment such as griddles or waffle irons were expensive, so many had to bake little cakes of ground cereal grain mixed with water or milk, and possibly flavoured with herbs or honey, directly into the embers of their fires. Baking these cakes required both an eagle eye and excellent judgement – the outside needed to be just scorched, and the inside fluffy and warm.

FANNIE FARMER AND THE CUP SYSTEM

At 30 years of age, Fannie Farmer enrolled in the Boston Cooking School as a mature student. Just five years later she was the principal. Her book *The Boston Cooking School Cookbook*, published in 1896, became a best seller, selling millions of copies and making her a household name, the Mrs Beeton of the USA.

One thing she is known for is being the inventor of the cup system of measurement: a system of measuring based on volume rather than a mix of weights and volumes. The truth is, the system wasn't in fact her creation, but mostly likely that of her teacher, Mary J. Lincoln. The idea was that by giving simple cup (and fractions of a cup) measures, it would help give those inexperienced in the kitchen a feel for cooking, helping them to become intuitive cooks. The trouble was that by giving cup measures, recipes become more standardised, and cooks became completely dependent upon them.

Fannie Farmer took this method and standardised measures further, taking a scientific approach and making them even more precise. She introduced the levelled spoon or cup measure to ensure total reproducibility and replaced vague phrases such as 'a knob of ...' or 'a piece as big a walnut' with precise volumes. She introduced some other rules: all meals and flours should be sifted – any dense lumps would lower one's accuracy – and then levelled with a knife. One cup was standardised to eight fluid ounces, or half a US pint, with Fannie recommending purchasing a set of graduated cups. These cups were easy to handle and much less expensive compared to weighing scales.

The system does break down when measuring other ingredients like meat and fruit such as chopped apples, but nay-sayers are missing something here: these cups and accompanying measuring spoons (teaspoons and tablespoons) were standardised representations of body measures, and a cup was supposed to represent a handful; a tablespoon, a thumb-size; both of which make more intuitive sense than abstract, and difficult to estimate, weights. Add that to the fact that in the nineteenth century, most measures of large amounts of grain, flour or oatmeal were measured in bushels (around 35 litres), so folk were certainly more used to handling volume over weight.

And so it caught on, and other countries adopted the method. In the US one cup is half a pint, but there was problem. A UK pint is twenty fluid ounces, compared to a US pint of sixteen, so the cups were not compatible. This caused great confusion, and special UK versions had to be made to account for this. In countries used to metric measures, such as New Zealand, a system was created where a metric cup was 250 millilitres (a quarter of a litre). The cup system broke down outside of the USA, and standardisation was needed. By the twelfth (1979) edition of Fannie's book, the editors had realised the issue, and included metric measures as well as US cups in the recipes, their 'purpose [being] to familiarise you with the system that Europeans have been using for years because metrics are bound to become an integral part of our kitchen language'.[14] However, the cup system is still very popular, and shows no signs of disappearing, and with the internet and more UK home cooks wanting to make authentic US recipes, and with proponents of the system such as Nigella Lawson, they are becoming increasingly popular in the UK. One of the things the cup system is particularly useful for is measuring the ingredients for griddlecakes, and Fannie's recipes are all excellent. Her recipe from the twelfth edition for fluffy pancakes is my go-to when I am hankering for proper US-style pancakes dripping with butter and maple syrup. The breakfast of champions!

CRUMPETS AND MUFFINS

What would you say is the difference between a crumpet and a muffin? I don't think I'm being in any way controversial when I say muffins* are bread-like in the centre (their name originating from the Old French word *moufflet*, meaning soft); cut out into circles or rolled into cakes; cooked on a bakestone; and dusted with semolina. Whereas crumpets are made from a pourable batter like a pancake (the word crumpet likely comes from the Welsh word for pancake, *crempog*); poured into rings; also cooked on a bakestone; slightly rubbery in texture, especially prior to toasting; have characteristic bubble holes on their top side. And let's not forget the pikelet, essentially a crumpet cooked without a ring, producing a large, hole-pocked pancake.

What I have described are modern factory-made versions, the traditional recipes now being almost entirely forgotten. This is what Elizabeth David wrote of the two in her classic book *English Bread and Yeast Cookery* (1977): 'crumpets, or at least travesties of them, can still be bought in England' and, 'Sainsbury's sell packets of a thing they *call* a muffin.'[15] But then she poses the following questions:

What is the difference between them? Which have holes, which are baked in rings? Which are made from a pouring batter, which from a soft dough ...? Is

---

* These are known as English muffins in the United States. Annoyingly, we don't call American muffins American muffins, just muffins, which are cakes, and not to be confused.

a pikelet the equivalent of a muffin or of a crumpet? Should muffins and/or crumpets be made from identical ingredients? If so, what are they? Flour, yeast, water and salt? Or flour and yeast plus milk, fat and eggs? Or flour, fat and eggs with a chemical raising agent?

She goes on to say 'anyone who knows the answers to more than two or three of these queries is wiser than I'. Today the answers to her questions are fairly straightforward, but then you look at the older recipes. The following two are both from the same 1914 book, *Cookery for Every Household* by Florence B. Jack, and use the same bubbly batter. To make crumpets: 'Heat a girdle, and grease it with butter; drop on to it of the mixture, and brown first on one side and then on the other.' That, I'm sure you'll agree, is a pikelet. Okay, let's see how to make muffins: 'Grease some rings, and place them on a hot greased girdle; half fill them with the mixture, cook and brown them on the other side.' Now that is a *crumpet*!

There is confusion here because the muffins of the nineteenth and early twentieth century were quite a different beast compared to today's supermarket offerings, because they were made from a yeasted batter so liquid and delicate they had to be proved on a layer of flour and were so fiendishly tricky to make that they could only be done by hand, and a well-trained one at that. Here are some instructions from *Law's Grocer's Manuel*, 1895:

get ready a tray, spread it with flour about 2½ [inches] in depth, make impressions in the flour with a small breakfast cup, take portions of the light dough out with a large spoon and put them into the flour impressions to rise; make the muffin stone hot, let them cook on it a few minutes, pass the palette knife under, turn them over ... and bake likewise, keeping them of a light colour.[16]

In an age of factory food this baking method has gone by the wayside, their mixture thickened into a dough that can be rolled and stamped out on a production line. So a muffin was almost a crumpet but not quite a bread, a spoonable dough hovering between two states producing a muffin honeycombed with holes, invisible until cut into. I now see why Ms David was so terse about the supermarket variety.

A WORLD OF FLATBREADS

There is a great variety of flatbreads and griddlecakes, made from diverse grains and flours, leavened and not. Despite their variety, what brings them together isn't just the fact they are baked on griddles, skillets, bakestones or hearthstones, but because they are quick to make, and are not dependent upon high-gluten – and therefore more expensive – flours; because of this, flatbreads are 'a major source of nourishment around the world'.[17]

The Chinese have spring onion pancakes, the USA Johnny cakes. Then there's the delicious maize-based Colombian *arepa* eaten with eggs and cheese, and of course Mexico's

45

tortilla, an export found right across the Western world today. Brazilian crêpes are made from tapioca flour and have a characteristic 'gummy' bite.* In Europe there is the Norwegian potato cake *lefse*, and the Italian *carta di musica*, a paper-thin semolina pancake. I could go on.

From the perspective of the British, its empire building and mixing of nations and cultures worldwide (whether they liked it or not), combined with the immigration of individuals of the ex-empire's Commonwealth in the mid-twentieth century to the UK, resulted in a whole range of foods, including flatbreads, becoming part of its food culture. When the first curry houses opened, British patrons preferred a slice of bread and butter with their curry but were soon coaxed away from their white sliced and toward North India's *chapati*. Traditional chapatis are made from wholewheat (wheat has been grown in India for around 8,000 years). The dough is rolled out and dry-fried on a *tava*, a large round griddle, slightly concave in shape. Of course, chapatis are just the tip of the iceberg: there are *paratha*, essentially chapati cooked in ghee; thin *dosa*, filled with aloo Masala (spiced potato), popular in Southern India. Then there is *roti*, a flatbread which seems to have travelled the furthest around the old empire. As Indians emigrated (often against their will or by being hoodwinked) to places such as Malaysia, South Africa and the West Indies, the *roti* went with them and was absorbed into the food culture. There is the straightforward *Saada roti* of Guyana and Trinidad, made

---

* Tapioca's gummy properties means it is often used in gluten-free flour mixes to provide a bit of spring.

from flour, water and baking powder, as well as their more luxurious *paraata roti*, made by rolling and folding the dough with oil to produce a delicious, decadent flaky flatbread. In Malaysia, huge, two-feet (sixty-centimetre) wide *roti canan* are cooked, their large shape achieved by applying centrifugal forces, i.e. by spinning the dough like a pizza base. Malaysians also enjoy yeasted *roti* pancakes, stuffed with peanuts, sugar and melted butter.

Possibly the most successful flatbread import is pitta bread: a versatile flatbread hailing from the Middle East, made from white or wholemeal flour, traditionally cooked on a hearthstone, though today it is usually baked in an oven. The secret to its success is the pocket that forms as it cooks, which can be filled with falafel and hummus, grilled lamb, or indeed anything that takes your fancy. The yeasted dough is rolled out into the familiar oval shape. It is important not to roll out too thinly, because when it hits the bakestone the outside crisps up, and inside the starch grains pop and gelatinise. When it is flipped and the other side cooks, the steam generated inside the pitta, which is still a starchy gel at this point, expands, ballooning the pitta, producing the pocket.*

I must mention the now-ubiquitous wrap, a flatbread that seems to be trying to displace pitta as the flatbread of choice, at least in the UK. These are very thin flatbreads of slightly yeasted dough that are used, in the main, to wrap

---

* This also happens when blind baking pastry and making biscuits, the remedy to which is to prick the dough all over with a fork. This is the reason why bought biscuits have their characteristic patterns of holes.

sandwich fillings. These thin, clammy – or worse, soggy – flatbreads, reminiscent of cadaverous skin, are a scourge on our otherwise excellent range of flatbreads. We need to elbow them out and open our arms to the wonderful diversity that exists in the wider world.

BREAD

Once the knowledge that difficult-to-digest cereal grains could be ground into flour, mixed with water and transformed into bread, all life became focused upon its production. Without bread, there would not be civilisation. Although a mixture of grains has been traditionally used, the production of wheaten bread in particular became the main focus of the Egyptians and then the Romans, and because of their vast empire, the pursuit was ever thus.

That bread is intrinsic to daily life is evident even in today's language. Workers earn 'dough' (or a crust), they are the breadwinner, and the work itself their bread and butter. When taxes increase people complain they are having 'the bread taken from their mouths'. There's an Italian saying that 'all troubles are easy with bread', and 'no pleasure is pleasant without bread'. Bread is at our sides through thick and thin. Unlike all other foods, it was eaten all year round and this is true since at least the Anglo-Saxon period. Tudor polymath Thomas Moffat wrote of bread, '[it] is never out of Season, disagreeing with no Sickness, Age or Complexion, and therefore truly called the Companion of Life.'[1] And indeed the word 'company' comes from the Latin *com*, meaning 'together', and *panis* meaning 'bread'; a company literally being a group of individuals that shares bread. Our language even shows us how society was structured by bread and bread-making. The word 'lord' comes from the Old English *hlaeford*, meaning 'loaf ward', the member of the community who distributes bread. The word 'lady' comes from *hlaefdige*, 'kneader of loaves'. In the feudal days of old, the community worked to provide the lord and his family with the raw materials for making bread; it was their payment to him in kind. He repaid them by giving them back some of the bread. This all sounds very nice, rather romantic, but it gives away the control the lord had over others: ovens were only allowed in the home of the lord, and baking was strictly controlled; and if the baking was controlled, so were the people who depended upon it.

Many Christian religious practices also revolve around bread: we ask God to 'give us our daily bread' in the Bible; whenever someone breaks bread, they are sharing and showing hospitality, extending the hand of friendship. Thomas Moffatt raises this point in *Health's Improvement*: 'in the Lord's Prayer, we ask for all bodily Nourishment in the Name of Bread, because Bread may be justly called the Meat of Meats.'* When receiving the Eucharist, bread is transformed into Christ's flesh, literal meat. Even Jesus's birthplace, Bethlehem, means 'house of bread'. A peasant in the Tudor period, when Moffatt was writing, may have only received the Eucharist once a year, and therefore it would

---

* See Moffat (1746) p.334. Meat in this context means any substantial food. For example, white meats were foods derived from milk.

be an important day, full of sombre gravity. Henry VIII, meanwhile, was receiving around five per day – he obviously required more forgiveness.

There were special breads throughout the Christian religious year: bread for harvest time, Christmas, Easter and Lent. That flour, salt and water could be transformed into bread was itself a miracle. Yeast, the living element of bread dough, was known as 'God's will' in the Middle Ages, and a prayer was said when it was added. Bread was magic, and it was protective. Because it was blessed, it could cure bewitchment, and divined information about the world around it. For example, a large hole in a loaf signified the baker was pregnant (a bun in the oven, you might say); dough wouldn't rise if there had been a death close by; and if loaves came out of the oven touching, marriage was afoot. This all sounds terribly twee, but it shows how important bread was to every individual in the Western world within a community, large or small, for the last ten centuries or so.

BREAD OVENS

We have seen that the earliest bakes were done on hearths and bakestones, but how did we progress from flat pieces of stone or iron to ovens? You might think that quite a leap of imagination was required, but it was not the case. Archaeologists have found evidence in Britain of a simple Bronze Age (c.2150 to 700 BCE) makeshift oven: a tall earthenware cooking pot sat among the embers of a fire, turned on its side, its mouth tilting slightly upwards, allowing heat to build up and circulate. The evidence for this? Pots discovered with scorch marks on their sides, not their bottoms, as is typical at other known sites. Another simple oven was made by placing dough on a bakestone and covering it with an upturned pot. Sometimes embers were shovelled around and upon it to make a simple Dutch oven. This method was still being used in the Middle Ages, when the building of ovens was tightly regulated; these cobbled-together ovens were invaluable and were able to generate enough steam inside to give unleavened bread dough at least a little lift.

This principle of covering baking food was refined into simple 'beehive' ovens: igloo-shaped domes with a small aperture at the front. Their origin lies in ancient Rome, but they were still being used in significant amounts in the latter half of the nineteenth century. The bread they make is excellent, and aside from a switch from clay to brick, the shape and design did not change for centuries. Even when fangled pastry ovens were installed in the seventeenth century, and iron ranges from the eighteenth, many stuck with the beehive. Says Eliza Acton in her *The English Bread-Book* (1859): 'Of all that are in common use amongst us at present, a brick oven, heated with wood, is generally best adapted to it.'[2] Even in the 21st century, a wood-fired oven is considered the very best piece of equipment for baking bread.

The oven was lit first with faggots (i.e. bundles) of dry drop wood and then larger pieces of wood, and as they burnt and turned red, they were spread over the oven floor, then swept out. A door was placed over the aperture (the 'stop-gap') to allow the heat to even out. This took several hours, and the temperature inside could reach a hellish 400 degrees Celsius, providing enough usable heat for 48 hours of baking. Achieving such temperatures required a lot of fuel and so baking day only occurred once a week or fortnight. Everything had to run like clockwork, and a great deal of skill was required to judge temperatures and baking times. The temperature was tested by throwing some flour or a piece of paper or dough into the oven and then seeing how long it took to burn. When the temperature was judged to be good, the oven floor was mopped to clean away ashes and provide steam, and the loaves of bread were swiftly thrust into the oven with the long-handled baker's paddle called a peel.

As the bread was baking, batches of other baked goods were prepared and lined up, each requiring a lower temperature to be baked successfully: next went in pastry, sweet buns and biscuits, then potted meat and fish, and finally custards were set in their blind-baked pastry cases. The last of the heat was utilised to dry grain, herbs and the kindling for next week's bake.

MEDIEVAL BREAD

In the early medieval period – the Anglo-Saxon Age – all of the major grains – rye, barley, oats and wheat – were being ground to make bread. Of these, the favourite was wheat, but whatever grain was used, bread was eaten with every meal. Indeed we get the word bread from the Old English *breadru*, and the word wheat from *hwǽte*, words that have barely changed in 1,500 years. One of the most important breads was made at Lammas ('loaf-mass') on the first day of August. It was special because the loaf would be made from the year's first ripe wheat harvested in the fields. The Lammas bread was not eaten, though; instead it was broken into quarters and crumbled in the four corners of the corn store, a wooden box large enough to stand in on short stilts, to bless and protect it, a sacrificial food. A more common bread was *bannuc*, a griddle bread made from any grains that were to hand.

After the Norman conquest, wheat was even more sought after and a variety of breads were made from it. Rough ground wholewheat was made, sliced and then dried to form trenchers, which were used by diners as a plate and cutting board. Some of the wheat was sifted, the bran removed and kept to make what was called *treatbread* and it was lowly bread indeed. The sifted flour was rolled up loosely into white sheets which were shaken over large troughs. As they were agitated, the whitest flour would eventually filter through the weave in the fabric into the trough. It was laborious, time-consuming work, and only the highest-status individual in the community ate the bread made from this white flour. This bread was called payndemayn or manchet bread.

There are many spellings of payndemayn, the root of this word being French, *pain demesne*, from the Latin *panum dominicum*, the lord's bread. The word appears in medieval manuscripts such as the fourteenth-century *Forme of Cury*. It was 'the lord's bread' because the small bread rolls – weighing in at around only 200 grams – were so precious that only the lord would receive one. Manchet is believed to be a contraction of the word payndemayn – *main* – and *cheat*, the name for another, similar bread made from refined flour that wasn't quite as white as the really good stuff. *Main* and *cheat* eventually became *manchet*.

There are mentions of this bread all over, but there are no real recipes from the Middle Ages. We have to wait for the age of the Tudors and Stuarts to get an idea of what they were like. Gervase Markham's recipe in *The English Huswife*, written in 1615, is one of the first to provide us with a good amount of detail as to how they were made, instructing us to take the risen dough and 'mold it into manchets, round, and flat, scotch [cut] about the wast to give it leave to rise, and prick it with your knife in the top, and so put it into the Oven, and bake it with a gentle heat'.[3] He 'pricks' the tops so that they don't rise too much in the oven.

The small loaf would be cut by the lord's server as described here in the *Boke of Keruynge* (*Book of Carving*) written in 1513: 'take a lofe in your lyfte hand. & pare y lofe rounde aboute than cut the over cruste to your souverayne, and cut the nether crust … & touch the lofe no more after it is so served.'[4] The 'over crust', being considered the best part, was eaten by the lord, and the rest divided up and given to whomever he pleased. This is the origin of the idiom 'the upper crust' we sometimes use when referring to the upper classes.

THE MIRACLE OF YEAST

These days we are all very familiar with the existence of wild yeasts and sourdough starters, and we must presume that the first leavened doughs were discovered quite by accident, by leaving dough or batter to naturally ferment. It seems that humans have been leavening their bread with yeasts for a good 6,000 years.

Lactic-acid producing bacteria dwells in flour, and so grows in the fermenting dough alongside wild yeasts, to make a 'sour-dough'. Not everyone likes their bread tasting sour, and a different method for producing yeast in large amounts was realised. It didn't come from batter or dough, but from the froth bubbling away on the surface of fermenting ale vats. This active yeast left no sour taste and was able to leaven the bread much more quickly than the slow-acting wild yeasts. The froth, called barm, was scraped off and added to bread dough. This link is an ancient one, and in towns, the bakery was always built next to the brewery. The earliest example of a brewery and bakehouse working together like this has been found in ancient Egypt, 2,000 years ago. Because this method of leavening dough was discovered so early, it is thought by some historians that the British never had a culture of making sourdoughs; with their love of ale, it was barm-leavened bread all the way. 'As we brew so must we bake' went the old English saying. The link is reflected in language: in Northwest England bread rolls are called barm cakes, and if we see someone behaving in a frenetic way, some of us might call them barmy.

No one knew that it was the action of yeasts that caused the dough to rise, it was deemed magic, a daily blessing from God Himself. It wasn't until the mid-nineteenth century that it came to light that all the hard work was being done by a microscopic fungus. Yes, a fungus, not a plant or a bacterium as some people think. Fungi cannot photosynthesise and have to find and ingest their food in order to live and reproduce. Yeasts assimilate starches and sugars and metabolise them into energy. If there is oxygen around, the sugar is converted into carbon dioxide and water; if there is no oxygen around it makes carbon dioxide and alcohol instead – this is why yeast is used to brew beer and wine. From the baker's point of view, it is the carbon dioxide that is the important thing, because it is this gas that, given time, forms the bubbles in the gluten-rich, elastic bread dough. If left to ferment slowly, yeast produces other, aromatic substances, giving the bread more flavour.

There is a problem with ale barm, and that is it is a living, dynamic gloop, which if left standing, quickly dies. The first commercially viable yeast was German or 'compressed' yeast. It is what we call today 'fresh yeast', and it can be bought cheaply from traditional bakeries if you ask nicely. It is made by growing yeast in water and molasses then extracting and compressing it. It keeps in the fridge for up to a week, and to get it going again, it is mixed into flour and water to make what is known as a sponge. A way of drying the yeast and sending it into a dormant state was devised in the 1920s, to make dry active yeast. To wake it up, it had to be creamed with warm water and a little sugar. It was a great step forward, but the yeast was temperamental and didn't necessarily survive its drying ordeal. It wasn't until the 1970s that instant yeast was devised – a fast-dried yeast that could be mixed straight into a dough with the other dry ingredients. Instant yeast is now the yeast of choice for many bakers, with the likes of Paul Hollywood and Raymond Blanc extolling its virtues.

SOURDOUGH STARTERS

The eating and baking of sourdough bread is something seen as a fairly new and fashionable way of leavening and flavouring bread, at least in the UK, a method that harnesses the powers of naturally occurring wild yeasts, already found in flour, to leaven the dough. Foodies and artisans nurture their wild starters and enjoy the sour flavour – caused not by yeasts, but by lacto-bacteria – and they wax lyrical over the chewy, open textures and the satisfying, cracking crust. Others deride it: a fad bread with a nasty sourness, a texture that makes eating it laborious, and a crust so hard and jagged that it will take the skin off the roof of your mouth. What's enjoyable about that!? Each to their own, I suppose. There are real benefits, though: the community of microbes produce nutrients not usually present in wheat flour such as essential amino acids and vitamins, and they digest the gluten proteins, making the bread in turn more digestible for our gut.

Benefits aside, those who dislike it are keen to point out that Britain has never had a sourdough bread culture in the first place. On the other hand, sourdough lovers say that it is the purest form of bread making, an almost elemental method of leavening one's bread, and a method by which we all made our bread at one point. The reality of the situation is that sourdough bread has been made in the British Isles certainly as far back as the Anglo-Saxons and probably in prehistory too. By the Victorian era, sourdough bread was deemed undesirable. Eliza Acton said rye flour is 'a coarse meal fermented by a leaven which is an unfavourable mode of fabricating it, because rye has a tendency to pass quickly into what is termed the acetous stage of fermentation [which must be] skilfully managed, to prevent the bread of it from acquiring an acid taste'.[5] It won't surprise you to hear that rye flour is considered the best for making sourdough starters. Another Victorian baker, Robert Wells, observed that a natural leaven is used in Cumbria to make a type of wholemeal bread, which, he reckons, 'always has a rank sour taste, and not to be compared with yeast-made bread'.[6]

These writers may not like the sour flavours, but it turns out that there are many examples of the British baking with sourdough cultures and batters: the Cornish used to make sourdough barley 'kettle bread', Scots made sour-scones, and the English made sourdough 'cheat' bread right into the era of the Stuarts. The latter, while being nutritious (it was made with a large proportion of bran), was certainly not prestigious. And here lies the issue; it all comes down to class and social standing. Dough made with brewers' yeast was associated with towns and cities, or with larger houses that could brew and bake their own ale and bread; sourdoughs, made by keeping back a proportion of dough today to use to leaven the dough tomorrow, became associated with rural communities and the peasant class. In France, however, where peasant food is revered, their *pain de campagne* – a countryside bread made in the way just described – is considered the pinnacle of bread perfection.

It turns out that you can dial up or down the sour flavours in naturally fermented bread to match your own tastes. Sourdough starters of the San Fransisco kind are usually made to a ratio of around three parts flour to five parts water, which favours growth of lacto-bacteria, but if one makes a starter with five parts flour to three parts water, yeasts are favoured, and the bacteria grow only slowly. This is the method used in France and was common across Britain; a naturally leavened bread with just enough acidity to enhance the natural flavours of wheat flour. Bring it back, I say.

THE NEED TO KNEAD

To knead a dough is to stretch it, roll it up, fold and turn it, and it takes just a little practice before the movement feels natural. When it's done only briefly, it brings together the ingredients of a dough, mixes them evenly and smooths it out. Bread, biscuit and pastry doughs are all kneaded to achieve this. But it is with bread dough that kneading is continued for several minutes – for here it serves a second purpose; to change the way gluten molecules are distributed within the dough, turning it from an amorphous blob of mixture into a podgy, round, springy ball of dough. But what exactly is gluten and what is going on inside bread dough that causes this change?

'Gluten', wrote Eliza Acton in her *The English Bread-Book* of 1859, 'is the substance ... that gives to wheat its superior value to every other kind of grain ... and renders the flour derived from it easily convertible into light, elastic dough.'[7] It is an insoluble protein, and it was first studied in the 1740s. Scientists didn't know what proteins were then, but it was observed that if some kneaded dough was manipulated further in water, the bulk of it dissolved or dissipated into the liquid, leaving behind a white, gummy, stretchy substance. This is gluten.

Proteins are polymers of simpler amino acids, of which there are over twenty types. They can form complex shapes and are handy molecules to have around, especially with respect to structure. Gluten is actually made up of two different proteins. One is a long, spiral-shaped molecule not unlike a very long slinky spring. When a dough is first mixed, these long molecules are scattered higgledy-piggledy. Kneading brings order to chaos by stretching out the springs and causing them to align, giving the dough strength. At the same time, the second, much smaller molecule, inserts itself between the long molecules, bringing them together while at the same time allowing them to move independently of each other, rather like ball bearings, making the dough more cohesive and stretchy at the same time. Strong bread flour can contain as much as 15 per cent gluten (compared to soft plain flour, which contains 8 to 10 per cent gluten). The salt in the dough, aside from adding flavour, tightens the proteins further, making the dough even more cohesive.*

The structural effects of gluten can be lessened. One way is by enriching the dough with butter, sugar or eggs. Some sweet-bun doughs are nigh-on impossible to knead with the hands and feel like they will never turn from sticky glue to plump dough ball. Electric mixers come in very handy at this point. Another way is to reduce the amount of gluten in the dough; in a fermenting sourdough mixture, bacteria eat the gluten, digesting it over the space of several hours (or days). This explains why sourdoughs must be proved in baskets – freeform sourdough loaves will just flatten out into round puddles of dough as they prove. That factory-made bread is fermented very quickly and without bacteria and is made with very refined white flour is one of the reasons cited for the recent uptick in the number of people finding they have gluten intolerances. Gluten is also found in rye, barley and oats, though from a baking perspective, they all behave as though they contain none at all. This is because the long molecules are too short to form any effective structure. Gluten is gluten, though, and if you have an allergy, you will still become ill after eating bread made from any of these grains.

---

* This effect is obvious if you ever make Italian meatballs: a mixture of protein-rich minced meat and raw eggs. As soon the mixture is seasoned with a good amount of salt, the mixture feels different in your hands: everything tightens up, helping the meatball stay together as it cooks.

WHAT'S YOUR LOAF?

In order to understand which flour has been used to make a loaf of bread, you really have to use your loaf just to get around the terminology – is brown bread the same as wholemeal? Is a farmhouse loaf made by hand, and has it even seen a farm in its metaphorical life? It's a difficult terrain to manoeuvre. Unfortunately, words like *farmhouse, hand-finished* and, sadly, *artisanal* have no real meaning in the modern world of food labelling. Today, it is best to ask your baker about the flours they use, and to check out the ingredients list if you are buying flour to make bread at home. In the case of bread, one thing is for certain: if it has been bought in a supermarket, even if from their in-store bakery, it is factory made, and so corners have been cut, too much water added, and the Chorleywood process applied – a process in which high-speed kneading machines make bread from scratch in just two hours. Even supermarket so-called sourdough breads are flavoured artificially. To help make things clearer, let's have a look at the most common bread flours and the breads made from them.

First up, wholegrain bread or flour: here the wholegrain has been 'extracted' in the milling process. This is the most nutritional flour, and it makes delicious, if rather heavy bread. There should be nothing on the ingredients list on the packet of wholegrain flour other than 100 per cent wholegrain flour. If wholegrain bread is purchased from a supermarket, it will have various additives, such as soy flour, to give it some shelf life. The bread can still be sold as 100 per cent wholewheat despite the fact soy flour is present: the reason being the

100 per cent wholewheat only applies to the wheat flour itself, not the soy flour, because it is added as an 'improver' as opposed to a main ingredient.

Brown bread is an umbrella term for any bread that is, well, brown. Wholemeal bread is brown bread, but so is farmhouse which is around 85 per cent extraction, meaning that 85 per cent of the whole grain has been included in the final bagged flour, most coarse elements removed, elements which also contain the most nutrition. This is enough to warrant most brown breads or bread flours to be artificially fortified with nutrients. Many supermarket brown breads are suspiciously soft and plumptious – a dead giveaway that the flour used to make it has had much of the good stuff taken away. One type of brown bread or bread flour you can be less suspicious of is of the malted kind. Here wholegrains have been germinated so that they begin to break down the stored starch into maltose sugar, the perfect energy source for a growing seedling. Once germinated, they are dried, toasted and ground. The malted wholegrain is then added to brown bread flour. It makes delicious bread. White bread flour is usually of 72 per cent extraction, despite the fact that the endosperm makes up 85 per cent of the wheat berry. This over-extraction is required because the separating of the bran from the endosperm is not perfect – hence the common use of bleaching agents. If you can, always buy unbleached white flour. We love white bread not because of its flavour, but for its comforting pillow-like texture, but many key nutrients have been lost. It has been law in the United Kingdom since 1941 to fortify white bread flour with calcium, iron and B vitamins. It seems odd to remove a whole suite of nutrients only to add a selection of them later, but this is the world in which we live.

When I make bread at home, I use a mixture of 100 per cent wholemeal and strong white flour. This way I can ensure that the bread made from it will have that spring we all desire plus the entire range of wheat's nutrients at the same time.

PIZZA

Ah, pizza! A cornerstone of the Western diet that manages to corner both the junk food and the artisan craft food market. Pizza, and its history, hit the headlines in 2023 when an image of what looked very like a pizza topped with what looked like a whole white cheese and some kind of fruit was discovered in Pompeii. The painting shows it sat on a silver tray accompanied with red wine and fresh fruit. But it is not a pizza because, according to a BBC article in 2023, it 'lacks the ingredients to be technically called a pizza'.[8] One of those ingredients is tomato, a New World food. It has been decided that the one true pizza is the Neapolitan – i.e. Naples – pizza, and anything else is merely a pretender, because in 2017 UNESCO made it a food with World Heritage Status. Only two sets of toppings are allowed: Marinara (tomatoes, garlic, oregano and oil) or Margherita (tomatoes, mozzarella, basil and oil).* Less is more when it comes to proper pizza it seems, and pizza aficionados get rather angry when they see pizzas piled with toppings. 'A pizza with everything', wrote Elizabeth David, 'is just what I don't want.'[9] A lot of heavy ingredients prevent the dough from puffing up, creating a very soggy bottom.

However, the world of food history is rarely straightforward, and a few others claim to be the true creators of the pizza. Romans reckon that their pizza topped with oil-stewed onions and oregano is the first, and that the Neapolitan is just 'a fanciful upstart',[10] whereas the folk of Armenia say they got there first with their baked flatbread topped with minced lamb, herbs and spices. Pizzas can be baked in any oven, but the best are cooked in super-hot wood-fired brick ovens, invented by the Romans and, some might say, never bettered, something impossible to replicate in the domestic kitchen. It's great that people become so passionate about their food traditions, but pizza, like any other 'traditional' food, is forever in flux and there is very rarely a 'true' original. Wherever pizza has travelled it has changed, adapted. From my personal point of view, peak pizza was reached in the South of France with its *pissaladière*, a flatbread topped with tomato sauce, black olives and lashings of salted anchovies. Even quiches are a likely cousin of the pizza; before the second half of the twentieth century, they were made with a base of yeasted bread dough and baked in a tin, not unlike an

---

* The latter was apparently invented in 1889 when a Napoli chef created it for a visiting Queen Margherita. Use a degree of caution with these stories, they are almost always untrue.

American pizza pie. And if you are thinking that if anything, quiches really belong to tarts and pies, you might be right, but it turns out that in the Italian language, the word pizza, until recently, meant anything pie or flatbread like. This makes *pizza pie* a somewhat tautologist term, but all of this mess also shows just how malleable and mobile food traditions really are. So don't worry if food snobs deride you because your favourite pizza is covered in pineapple chunks or smothered with barbecue sauce, it's your tradition, and that's the only one that really counts.

ITALIAN BREADS

The pizza isn't Italy's only flatbread enjoyed around the world, there are also focaccia and ciabatta. Focaccia, that fluffy, tender and hole-pocked bread baked with lots of olive oil and studded with olives is certainly one of the world's most delicious breads. Its origin is in antiquity, starting life as a hearthbread, indeed it gets its name from the Latin for hearth, *focus*. It owes its delicious texture, in part, to the high water content of the dough. A regular white British loaf is made from a dough of 60 per cent hydration, meaning that the dough is made up of 60 parts water to 100 parts flour. Focaccia dough is of 65 per cent hydration, making a dough that is sticky, floppy and hard to handle and knead – much patience is required to achieve a workable dough. If you do ever make one, don't be tempted to add more flour. To make things easier to knead, it pays to let the just-mixed dough sit and absorb some of the water for fifteen minutes or so. Before it goes in the oven it needs some olive oil brushed over it, some sea salt flakes sprinkled over it, and some olives pushed into it. Don't go overboard; like a pizza, less is more when it comes to toppings.

Ciabatta dough is a different kettle of fish entirely; coming in at 80 per cent hydration, it is nigh-on impossible to handle. This high proportion gives it those characteristic large holes. Although it is sold as a traditional Italian bread, the ciabatta doesn't have the heritage of the focaccia, being invented in 1982, a time when Italy feared its own bread industry was being usurped by the popular, imported baguette. The ciabatta was Italy's response, and it was a great success. The word itself means carpet slipper, owing to its elongated, rather saggy shape, enhanced by the lashings of olive oil and crusty semolina coating. Its comparative youth shouldn't put you off, it is delicious and seems to have nestled itself into baking culture all over the Western world. It makes me think of the 1990s, when dipping it into balsamic vinegar was quite the sophisticated gastronomic experience.

Its coating of semolina flour isn't there to achieve a good crust, but because liquid dough is left to prove on a thick layer of the stuff – impressions are made in the coarse flour, and the runny pieces of dough are placed in them to prove. It's the only way to do it, anything else would cause them to stick. Once risen, they are gingerly placed on trays for baking. Baker Daniel Steven has some advice for the home cook with respect to ciabatta: he suggests 'you don't attempt it until you are a reasonably proficient baker, or it will make you feel disheartened'.[11] Recipes do crop up in cookery books, but often they are altered to make the process easier: proving in lavishly oiled tubs (even more messy) or by reducing the hydration, meaning you haven't made a ciabatta, but something else entirely. It is a task best left to the artisan bakers of the world.

SHAPING AND CUTTING

Once your bread dough has been thoroughly kneaded and is good and springy, it is time to let the dough rise until at least double its size. It's formed and tucked into a ball, popped back in a bowl and covered with a damp tea towel or cling film. It can take between 30 and 90 minutes, depending upon ambient temperature, and the amount and the vigour of your yeast. When risen, the dough is 'knocked back'. Some say to do this gently, leaving in as much of the captured air as possible, others say to give it a good, satisfying punch and let all of the carbon dioxide out. Either way, the dough can then be shaped, and whether it's baked on a tray or in a tin, the important thing to do is to get the surface of the dough good and taut so that when the dough rises again, its round shape is retained as it grows. To do this, gather the dough into a ball and on a very lightly floured worktop, make it even rounder by tucking your hands under it, twisting it slightly as you go. The tight ball of dough can be sat on a floured sheet and covered to prevent a skin from forming; a large clean bag is good for this, though bakers sometimes paint their dough with water to prevent it from drying out in the second rise.

The second rising is called proving because it 'proves' to you that the yeast is still working. Usually, this takes about a third of the time of the first rising. To tell whether your dough has proved enough, press the side gently with a lightly floured thumb; the indentation should spring back within a second or two. Now the all-important cuts can be made. This is where some folk bring out their razor-sharp blades and slash away, a method I have never got on with. I go instead for the more sedate and dependable serrated bread knife: one confident slash across the top, and another to make a cross; the weight of the knife itself is the only pressure you will need for success.

I have just described how to make a simple round cob loaf, but you could cut criss-crosses to make a college or Manchester loaf, or snip all over with scissors to make a hedgehog. Before you cut, you could sprinkle the top with flour, or paint your dough with water and sprinkle it with seeds. A tiger loaf is made by painting the shaped dough with sesame oil. You could make your dough into an elongated slug shape, tucking it down just at the sides, flouring and slashing diagonally several times to make a bloomer or pop it into a floured tin for a sandwich loaf. If you make your cut from one corner to its opposite, you have made a split tin.

Thrust your dough into a hot oven with a tray of boiling water sitting at the base (for those of us without a clay or brick oven) and bake until the bread sounds hollow when tapped and the crust is brown and crackling. There are hundreds of variations, but many agree that the trickiest is the cottage loaf.

COTTAGE LOAVES

'It is as hard to achieve the right shape and texture, crust and crumb, of an authentic cottage loaf as it is to reproduce true French baguette bread.' Elizabeth David[12]

The cottage loaf is a vintage British classic, and a bread unique to England. Most Brits have heard of them, but how many have ever clapped eyes on one in real life? If you are not familiar with one, a cottage loaf is made up of two cobs – i.e. ball-shaped loaves – stacked one on top of the other, the upper loaf being around half the size of the bottom one. The shape is curious, making even slicing difficult, and according to Elizabeth David, writing in her classic tome *English Bread and Yeast Cookery*, they are fiendishly difficult to make and impossible to reproduce at home. Unless you are Virginia Woolf, that is, who apparently made an excellent one. She used an oil cooker and with it tutored her cook, called Louise Mayer, to bake cottage loaves. Louise recounted in the book *Recollections of Virginia Woolf* (1972):

she could make beautiful bread ... I was surprised how complicated the process was and how accurately Mrs Woolf carried it out. She showed me how to make the dough with the right quantities of yeast and flour, and then how to knead it. Finally, she made the dough into the shape of a cottage loaf and baked it at just the right temperature. I would say that Mrs Woolf was not a practical person – for instance, she could not sew or knit or drive a car – but this was a job needing practical skill which she was able to do well every time. It took me many weeks to be as good as Mrs Woolf at making bread, but I went to great lengths practising and in the end, I think, I beat her at it.[13]

These unique loaves were invented in the early nineteenth century and a picture of one crops up in *Mrs Beeton's Book of Household Management* (1861). They were originally baked directly on the bottom of bread ovens like many cobs, muffins and breadcakes are still baked today. These ovens had no shelves, meaning one was rather restricted in the number of crusty cobs one could bake at a time. That's where the smaller upper loaf comes in; a second cob made without taking up extra precious space in the oven.

The tricky element in making a cottage loaf is to keep the top piece from falling off during proving and baking, and according to Ms David, it does need to lean slightly to one side like a jaunty hat. But you can't just sit one on top of the other, you have to *fix* it in place, by taking floured fingers and plunging them through the top *and* bottom cobs so that floured finger hits baking sheet two or three times. For it to work it must be done deftly and with confidence, but it is nowhere near as difficult to make as Elizabeth David says. Like everything, just willingness and a little practice are all that are required.

STICKY BUNS

There was once a great variety of delicious, sticky bread buns made from doughs enriched with fat, sugar, eggs and spices. They have been greatly reduced in number, and the only type familiar to us all today is the hot cross bun. A few regional specialities have hung on such as Yorkshire teacakes, Cornish splits, Devonshire chudleighs and Cornish saffron buns. Sticky buns became popular in Tudor times when spices and sugar were still very expensive, but nowhere near as pricy as they had been in the Middle Ages. Sticky buns enriched with butter and eggs and a small amount of sugar and spice became an affordable rare treat, at least to the middle classes.

Many believe buns such as these are something better bought than made. Enriched doughs are soft and sticky, making them difficult to knead, and the butter and sugar get in the way of gluten development, meaning they have to be kneaded for longer. However, in these days of domestic standing mixers with dough hooks, there has never been a better time to start making them at home again very successfully. As Jane Grigson wrote in *English Food* (1992):

Until you make spiced hot cross buns yourself, or well-sugared Chelsea buns, it is difficult to understand why they should have become popular. Bought, they taste so dull. Modern commerce has taken them over, and, in the interests of cheapness, reduced the delicious ingredients to a minimum – no butter, little egg, too much yellow colouring, not enough spice, too few currants and bits of peel, a stodgy texture instead of a rich, light softness. In other words, buns are now a doughy filler for children.[14]

Alas, she is correct – we've all become accustomed to factory buns and only a few of us have experienced the delight of a homemade sticky bun.

One popular regional bun is the famous Bath bun, which is said to have been invented by a doctor called William Oliver in the eighteenth century. After his patients visited the Roman baths, he would give them an enriched Bath bun. However, as W. Chambers wrote in his *Edinburgh Journal* of 1855, decades later, 'It was easier for ancient mariners to resist the temptations of the Sirens, than it is for a modern child to turn away from a Bath-bun',[15] and it was soon apparent that Oliver's plan was not working as expected when he realised his patients were getting rather portly. He withdrew the buns and replaced them with hard, dry water biscuits.

Another Bath invention is the Sally Lunn. The story goes that a young French immigrant landed in Bath in the eighteenth century and got herself a job in a bakery. It turned out her baking was excellent, and what was this woman called? Solange Luyan. The recipe went missing in the 1800s but was apparently found during the 1930s in a secret cupboard in her original home. The owner of the house then decided to open up the original Sally Lunn Tea Room. This is, of course, all complete nonsense. The most likely explanation is that *Sally Lunn* is a corruption of the French *solielune*, or 'sun-and-moon' cake.

We reach the peak of the sticky buns with the Chelsea bun: a delicious coil of bun dough filled with dried fruit, brown sugar and melted butter, and glazed with sugar syrup. There is nothing more delicious. They were invented in the early nineteenth century at the Chelsea Bun House, built close to Pimlico. It was very popular and was frequented by the spouse of King George II, Queen Caroline. They beat the now seemingly ubiquitous cinnamon bun any day, and deserve reassessment and a comeback.

HOT CROSS BUNS

Hot cross buns have a very long history, going back to the Anglo-Saxon period, and may even be a hangover of the Roman occupation of Britain. They are embedded in folk tradition and although they were not originally spiced, they were probably enriched with milk, butter or egg. What they certainly did have was a cross; cutting the cross dispelled bad spirits and gave the buns supernatural powers:[*] drinking the water that hot cross buns were steeped in was restorative. The buns could never go mouldy or stale[†] and were hung from the rafters for good luck. That's the *cross* taken care of, but what about the *hot*? We don't actually eat them hot that often. They were simply called cross

---

[*] Cutting a cross also ensures a more even bake.

[†] This is certainly true in my house because they are not around long enough to get stale or mouldy.

buns, until that famous nursery rhyme was written sometime in the eighteenth century, taken from the common cry of London street sellers to emphasise their freshness:

Hot cross buns, hot cross buns!
One ha'penny, two ha'penny, hot cross buns!
If you have no daughters, give them to your sons,
One ha'penny, two ha'penny, hot cross buns!

In more strict Lenten times, when all animal products had to be avoided, these enriched buns were still eaten, despite containing butter and eggs, the reason being that bread of any kind was allowed during times of fasting. They were eventually banned from sale during the reign of Elizabeth I because everyone was getting fat at a time of great fasting. An exception was made, and it became law that they could only be made and sold on Good Friday. Ever since, they have been associated with this particular day. And – let me tell you – people really loved it when it came round to Good Friday; in London at the Chelsea Bun House, there was almost a riot on Good Friday 1792 because of the sheer number of people clambering in the massive queues to buy one.

PUMPERNICKEL, RYE AND ERGOT

Bread made from rye flour has, historically, been rather unpopular in the British Isles, despite the fact it tastes good, and the cereal grows well in its warm, damp climate. Tasty as it may be, it lacks elastic gluten, producing a dense loaf, and is therefore considered inferior. To overcome this in the Middle Ages, it was mixed with wheat flour to make maslin bread, but as soon as it was possible, it was ditched for springy all-wheat bread.

Rye breads are much more popular in Northern and Eastern Europe where rye grows extremely well. It is often flavoured with caraway, dill or cumin seeds. The best-known of these breads is German *pumpernickel*, introduced to Britain by Jewish immigrants: it is a very dense sourdough bread made from rye only and has a very long shelf life; it is often found in health-food shops. It is made by mixing rye flour, whole rye grains and leftover stale pumpernickel with salt and water. After fermenting the resulting batter for three days it is shaped and baked in a slow oven: it was invented to utilise the residual heat of the wood-fired ovens. Because it is made from wholemeal rye flour and whole rye grains, and is naturally fermented, it is considered to be very good for one's digestion. It seems that our own gut bacteria enjoy the bread too, causing flatulence, hence its name: *pumper* means to stink or to fart and *nickel* is a reference to Old Nick, the Devil, so it is a bread that makes you fart like the devil.

But rye flour can be dangerous. A poisonous fungus called ergot, which also likes warm and wet climes, can grow on rye plants. There have been several outbreaks of ergot poisoning, which is caused by a variety of alkaloids, each having a different effect. One causes the blood vessels of the limbs to constrict, causing the extremities to turn black – in medieval Europe, this was known as St Anthony's Fire. In extreme cases, they became gangrenous and fell off. Another alkaloid causes the muscle of the uterus to constrict, giving the sensation of going into labour. One, which is chemically very similar to LSD, causes psychoses and hallucinations. The poet William Blake once had a psychotic episode after eating infected rye bread, causing him to hallucinate angels sitting in trees while on an afternoon stroll. It has even been hypothesised that ergot delirium was the real cause of the apparent witchcraft 'observed' in the North American town of Salem in 1692. The descriptions of events provided in the Salem Witch Trials are conducive to psychosis brought on by ergot alkaloids, and it just so happened that the weather during the growing seasons of 1691 and 1692 was perfect for the growth of ergot. Could this community, dependent upon rye bread, be victims of a group psychosis?

Events such as these have often been blamed on the communities not making sourdough rye loaves, the community of microbes preventing the growth of the fungus. As it turns out, this is not the case: ergot poisoning doesn't happen very much today, but this is not because of the return of the sourdough loaf, it is because rye flour is meticulously sampled before it is sold to factories, groceries and bakeries.

FRENCH BREAD

The French have been lauded for centuries for their approach to cookery and gastronomy, and of course, this includes their breadmaking. The best known of the French breads is the baguette, but it's a relative newcomer, not really popular until the nineteenth century. Before then it was all about the rustic *pain de campagne*, the olive-oil-laden *fougasse* or the ring-shaped *couronne*, all sculpted and precisely cut. Beautiful they may be, they were not that dissimilar to British breads, the long, free-form *bâtard* with its diagonal cut is essentially a British bloomer with a more romantic-sounding name.

French bread recipes have appeared in English cookery books since the seventeenth century. In Robert May's *The Accomplisht Cook*, first published 1660, he tells us how 'To make French bread the best way'. He uses fresh ale barm, a mix of milk and water and 'the whites of six new laid eggs well beaten', which are made into 'roules' and baked.[16] What the eggs do is uncertain, the inclusion stumped even Elizabeth David, who said 'I am not sure what the egg whites do in the bread; whatever it is produces very good results.'[17] Similar recipes crop up right through to the early nineteenth century.

However, when we think of French bread now, we think of the baguette. This icon of baking requires an oven to be injected with steam as it bakes, a method learned from the Viennese. The steam gelatinises the surface starches of the dough, which, once the steam has dispersed, caramelises to a beautiful cracking crust. The other difference is in the flour itself, because it contains much less gluten than regular bread flour, being a mix of around 20 per cent strong bread flour and 80 per cent plain flour, which according to many gives it better flavour, but less of a rise and larger holes; unlike in Britain, where 'the volume of the loaf is achieved at the expense of the savour' as Elizabeth David once waspishly put it.[18] However, it is this low gluten that gives the bread its short shelf life, and bakeries produce several batches per day. This made the baguette a luxury item, especially because the equipment required to bake it made it impossible to make at home, unlike the homelier country breads. Indeed, many French folk, especially those living in the countryside, call the baguette Vienna bread, and refuse to acknowledge it as French bread at all. To them French bread is *pain de campagne*.

Outside of France, the baguette is viewed as the epitome of French bread, and it has become one of the country's most significant culinary exports. It took over the world in the 1980s and is now found in every train station sandwich unit, furnished with pizza topping or garlic butter in the freezer aisle of the supermarket, sold off in great numbers for next to nothing of an evening. It is so common now that this once most revered of breads has simply bred contempt, so removed now is it from its luxuriant origins.

BAGELS AND PRETZELS

When the Jewish people of central Europe migrated to several places around the world in the Great Diaspora in the nineteenth century, many found themselves on the shores of the New World, in particular New York. It is here that two traditional breads spilled out from the Jewish communities to be enjoyed throughout North America, and then the Western world. Two bread stalwarts: bagels and pretzels.

The word bagel is a German-Yiddish one that simply means 'ring'. Its origin seems to be in South Germany, but bagels became popular in neighbouring Poland too, and it is the Polish Jews who brought the bagel to North America. In 1937 the first Bagel Bakers Union was founded, and now, less than a century later, the bagel business is worth $900 billion per year in the US alone.

Bagel dough is of low hydration for a bread, coming in at just 45 to 50 per cent, a stiff dough that restricts bubble size during fermentation and therefore the amount of rise during proving. This is counteracted by plopping it into 'violently boiling water for a matter of seconds before baking'.[19] This keeps a crust from forming too quickly once in the oven, allowing for a little more lift. It also gelates the surface starch a great deal, producing that signature chewy crust. The caramelisation on that crust is often enhanced by dipping the bagel dough into sugared, or honeyed, water. Bagels must be eaten fresh on the day they are baked, after that they should be toasted. Care must be taken that the dough is shaped properly; you must form a ring with a suitably large hole; you don't want it to fill itself in during the proving and baking process. To get the right size, cut a strip of dough, roll it and wrap it around a clenched fist, sealing the dough at your palm, removing any excess. This produces a ring of appropriate proportion.

The pretzel came to America a little before the bagel, the first recipe appearing in print in the 1820s. The word pretzel is a German one meaning 'little bracelet'. They are yeast-leavened but with a dough so stiff you could argue they are more of a biscuit. Pretzels are very dark in colour, and scattered liberally with salt crystals, making them a traditional accompaniment to beer. This is not the only type, and there is a whole tribe of different pretzels, some sweet, some definitely biscuits; but whatever the precise ingredients, they are all made in their classic knot shape.

Pretzels are made by making a sausage of dough that tapers at both ends, which is deftly, and magically it seems, lifted and twisted in a single motion to make a knot; quite a satisfying spectacle to see. The knots are then sprayed with a weak solution of sodium hydroxide (sometimes called lye). When it bakes the surface gelatinises and caramelises – just like a bagel – but the addition of that alkaline chemical creates an especially dark and delicious crust which looks particularly attractive if the dough is cut just before it goes in the oven. It is baked at a high heat briefly, and then the heat is turned down for a long bake, giving it that chewy, biscuit-bread texture. They make excellent teething rings for babies, salt crystals omitted.

CORNBREAD

With the discovery and colonisation of the New World by Europeans from the late-fifteenth century, many exciting new foodstuffs and ingredients were brought to the fore. From the story of baking's point of view, the most important of these was maize, which is made into cornbread, a food instilled in North America's food culture and identity. That maize is also called corn is somewhat confusing, but it made sense to the English colonists in the sixteenth century, who called maize 'Indian corn', the word corn being used as a catch-all term for the grains of any cereal crop since at least 1000 CE. The word 'Indian' was eventually dropped and maize became simply 'corn'.

By the time the colonists arrived, maize was already being cultivated by many groups of Indigenous American. They had actually originated in Central and South America, but moved north into what is now New Mexico by 3500 BCE, and into New England around 700 BCE. When the interactions between English colonists and Indigenous Americans were positive, cornmeal was valued and traded, and cornbread was taken to the colonisers' hearts. These maize-based batter puddings were enriched with milk or fats and lightened with eggs; it was impossible to make into loaves because maize contains no structural gluten, making them pudding-like in texture. Later they would be lightened by the action of yeast, as this recipe from the 1824 classic American cookbook *The Virginia Housewife* by Mary Randolph instructs:

CORN MEAL BREAD

Rub a piece of butter the size of an egg, into a pint of corn meal – make it a batter with two eggs, and some new milk – add a spoonful of yeast, set it by the fire to rise, butter little pans, and bake it.[20]

The bread may have been baked in a Dutch oven, a covered iron skillet or a range cooker. Later, baking powder and ground wheat were added to make the cornbread even lighter. Today, cornbread also contains sugar, making it somewhat cake-like and rather different from its humble beginnings.

Cornbread is extremely important from a cultural point of view: it has been made by so many communities at different times and in different ways that it is estimated there are 336 different names for it. These names are interesting because they often give away information about who was making it and why. For example, cornbread made by Indigenous Americans was called 'Indian stamp bread' by the new Americans; *johnnycake* is a griddlecake that can be easily made by the traveller, *johnny* being a contraction of the word 'journey'; *ashnanny* was a hearth cake baked in the embers of a fire; *crackling bread* contained chopped up crisply fried chitterlings (pigs' intestines). When wheat was grown in large amounts in North America, corn and cornbread became associated with enslaved peoples and the poor. This is given away in one of its other names, *bastard bread*, meaning in this case, 'false bread'. African slaves in the state of Maryland and their descendants made *hoecakes* from cornmeal, salt, water and lard. Because the majority of slaves were traded and set to work in the southern states, cornbread is associated with that area of America, soul food and their particular brand of generous hospitality. Cornbread's links with the poor extended across the Atlantic Ocean when maize and cornmeal were exported to Ireland in the nineteenth century, as a cheap source of carbohydrates to feed those caught in the terrible throes of the potato famine.

Today cornbread has shaken off its stigma and is – quite rightly – lauded as a cornerstone of American cuisine. It's just a shame that the colonising Europeans took so long to realise the fact.

ADULTERATION

Aside from the pleasure and delicious taste you get from baking your own bread you might think you are keeping your family in good quality 'pure' bread, baked as it should be, no corners cut. The quality and perceived purity of a homemade loaf far exceeds that of a plastic-wrapped supermarket loaf full of preservatives and raising agents. Such loaves are made by the Chorleywood process, an invention of the 1960s where dough, made with a lot of water and yeast, is mixed by high-speed kneading machines, producing bread that can be made from scratch in two hours flat. The dough is helped along by a suite of chemicals, some of which are rather nasty. For example, a chemical called azodicarbonamide – banned in the UK since 2016, but still allowed in US bread – adds bubbles to both bread dough and exercise mats.

You would think making your own bread sidesteps all of these chemicals, but you are most probably wrong: the chances are your bread flour contains several adulterants and additives. Indeed, folk have been adding foreign ingredients to flour for millennia, and for a variety of reasons. Even bakers in ancient Rome were accused of padding out their flour with chalk. In the eighteenth century, a pamphlet was published by an anonymous author (later identified as Mr Peter Markham) called *Poison Detected*, which let know that the addition of some chalk was merely the thin end of the wedge. He observed that 'our bread, the universal basis of the food of all ranks and ages of people, is mixed with most noxious and morbiferous matters'.[21] He declared that 'it is averred by a very creditable authority that sacks of old ground bones are not infrequently used by some'. Even worse, 'the charnel houses of the dead are raked to add filthiness to the food of the living'.[22] This is propaganda, but flour was frequently cut with cheaper white powders to bulk out the expensive white wheat flour, which by the eighteenth century everyone was demanding. The most common of these was alum, a bright-white mineral, which, aside from being a lightener, made the bread spongier, a so-called 'improver' for lower gluten wheat flours. It is not a poison, but it is very astringent, causing constipation as it passes through the gut, as well as abrasion of the teeth.

Flour could be mixed with less dubious adulterants such as potato starch or ground maize – not harmful, but not what you are expecting in your wheat flour – and with zero gluten content would probably force the trickster's hand to add a bit of alum just to get away with their tinkering. In her *English Bread-Book* (1859) Eliza Acton was up in arms about the blind-eyes that were being turned to this sort of thing, especially compared to France, where quality was king and adulterators were (according to her) 'whipped naked at the crossroads'.[23] Toward the end of the nineteenth century, things became even worse with the invention of the roller mill, which, unlike traditional mills, was able to both grind and sort flour into 'fractions', meaning pure white flour could be made extremely efficiently. But this flour is completely devoid of almost all nutrients other than starch and gluten. This type of milling quickly became the norm, and unless your bag of flour says it is stone ground (usually in proud lettering) then it has been ground by roller mill. Unhappy with the whiteness of the flour, manufacturers made it whiter still with the addition of sulphur or ozone in the nineteenth century, and then chlorine dioxide in the twentieth. White flour should be a natural, creamy colour; any flour (or bread) that is truly white should be viewed with suspicion and avoided.

Post the Second World War, the roller mills were so efficient that the government put forward the Flour Order, requiring that some of the nutrients stripped out by the roller mills were to be added back in: iron, vitamin B, nicotinic acid and calcium (in the form of chalk, just like the Romans!). Vitamin C was added for good measure. This order is still enforced today, and all flours, aside from those made with 100 per cent wholegrain, have to be fortified with these additives. So, unless you are milling and bolting your own white flour, or only baking with wholegrains, then, unfortunately, you are also consuming adulterants.

WARTIME BREAD

The British public's preference for the fluffiest, whitest daily bread – despite it being devoid of nutriment – was challenged in the Second World War, when the nation's flour and bread became controlled by the government. Bread wasn't rationed during the war; the government thought it would be too much for the populous to bear. Instead, a standard National Flour of 85 per cent extraction was to be offered to housewives and bakeries around the country. This flour was brown, and because the wheat it was made from was grown in Britain, it lacked the gluten the country had become very used to, producing a stodgier loaf, with very little spring. The country hated it, perhaps more because they were provided with no other choice. Things were made even worse when the flour was made to go further by the addition of cold mashed potatoes or potato flour to the mix. Potatoes grew well and abundantly in Britain, and housewives were urged to make less bread for their families, and so the Ministry of Food suggested potatoes as an appropriate adjunct to make the home-grown flour go much further. As a result, the bread was even more despised.

But whether you liked it or not, it had to be eaten, because during the time the country was at war it had become illegal to waste food, and bread – then as now – was the most wasted of foods. To tackle this, the Ministry of Food produced a set of posters and pamphlets to plant the issue of bread waste in the forefront of the housewife's mind, while trying not to alienate her. A 1944 leaflet declared: 'The housewife deserves a bouquet for the part she is playing in the War effort, but she is falling down on one thing – the daily waste of bread.' The leaflet goes on to say that the equivalent of 30 shiploads of bread per year were being wasted in homes across the country at a time when home-grown food was a very precious resource indeed. The ministry had done their homework and worked out that it was the last, rather stale, third of a loaf that got thrown away. This was their advice: 'When you get to the last three inches of your loaf, place it crumb side down on the bread board', thus keeping it from drying out. The loaf could then be sliced into fingers.

Curiously, it was only after the war had ended that flour and bread were rationed in Britain, a time that should have seen the country change back into a land of plenty now that trades routes and imports had returned to normal. And it would have been, were it not for a severe world shortage of grain crops. Bread therefore had to be rationed between 1946 and 1948, which just goes to show how fragile the world's globalised trade is. It can never be wholly predictable or dependable, something that has been made clear to us all since Russia's 2022 invasion of Ukraine, the breadbasket of Europe.

THE GREAT BREAD-ROLL DEBATE

It is one of the British Isles' most hotly debated topics, and I realise I am perhaps putting my neck on the line here just with this phrasing, but what do *you* call a bread (dare I say it) roll? According to the BBC Travel website, 'Everyone in the UK has an opinion on just what to call what is perhaps the most inoffensive foodstuff known to man.'[24] Yes indeed, and I am only using the term bread roll because it is the most popular one.

It's given that moniker because to make one, a ball of dough is rolled in a circular motion, tightening it up so that it rises round and plump in the oven. But I know which side my bread is buttered on, and I go for breadcake, a term that vies for second place with barmcake, closely followed by bap in fourth position.

Outside of these big hitters, there is quite the list – do any of the following ring true for you? We have cobs, muffins, morning rolls, butteries, Vienna rolls, bridge rolls, huffkins, stotties, oggies, scufflers and teacakes. According to the Our Dialects website there are twenty variations in name in England alone. Most remain regional: barmcakes are restricted to Northwest England, especially Greater Manchester, cobs in the Midlands. Then there are the hyper-regional huffkins (Kent), scufflers (Leeds) and muffins (Oldham).

Why all of this variation in name? Well, it demonstrates just how strongly our food identities are linked to our regional roots, despite the fact that today we are more connected and move around more than ever before. However, we have to be very careful here because these terms are not always interchangeable and the differences not purely linguistic; these are not different words for the same food at all – okay, some may be just different shapes (rolls *versus* finger) or textures (crusty cob *versus* soft bap), but stotties, popular in the very Northeast of England, are enriched with milk and are seasoned with white pepper; teacakes in Yorkshire are enriched with lard; delicious buttery rowies from Scotland are enriched with butter and lard and have a slightly flaky texture; and Oldham muffins are baked on the bottom of the oven and have more similarities with bakestone breads than regular bread rolls. These subtle differences are very important, more important than names, I would argue, and it just goes to show that – as is so often the case with apparently simple foods – the devil is always in the detail.

CHRISTMAS BREADS: STOLLEN AND PANETTONE

Once upon a time during Yuletide, a variety of traditional regional Christmas breads were baked across the British Isles, but now preparations such as Cumbrian Christmas bread or Guernsey *gâche*, all enriched with butter, eggs and flavoured with dried fruit, candied peel and spices, have all been ousted by Christmas cake. This is a great shame, and looking out to continental Europe where Christmas breads are still alive and well, we can see what we are missing out on: Swiss *Grittibänz*, little brioche men complete with plaited brioche scarves and hats; or Swedish enriched saffron buns known as *Lussekatter*; or Greek *Crisostomo*, enriched bread liberally flavoured with aniseed. These are obscure, but two breads have swept into British shops at Christmastime and been so successful that some people have become worried that the British Christmas cake may be usurped. What goes around comes around, I suppose. These breads are Italian *panettone* and German *stollen*.

The stollen we know is a speciality of the German city Dresden, with its delicious flaked almonds, dried fruit and vein of marzipan running through its length. Its name appears to derive from the word *stollo*, meaning post or support, such as the ones you might find in a mine, but how it links to an almondy bread is anyone's guess. The long tapering shape of the stollen is supposed to represent the infant Christ wrapped in His swaddling.

Panettone hails from Milan, and the origin of its name is even more dubious than stollen's: supposedly, a poor baker called Toni who, after hearing that his lord was without any Christmas bread to eat, made an enriched bread for him from the piece of sourdough he had put aside for his own family. Good old Toni. The lord finds it delicious, and names it *panettone* – Toni's bread – which is shared about the court, found delicious, really takes off and makes our Toni a rich man.

Whatever its origins, it is much beloved in Italy – the average family consuming two-and-a-half of them over the Christmas period – and they are certainly now part of the Christmas spread in Britain today. In 2023 the *Guardian* reported that sales of panettone were increasing year-on-year (there was a similar increase for stollen too). Like it or not, panettone does have a few things going in its favour over the British Christmas cake: it is nice and light (it is baked in steep-sided tins to give it height and lightness), it often comes in a nice tin, and it comes in a number of varieties like chocolate chip, making them the go-to for anyone who hates dried fruit, of whom there are many, and dried fruit haters do have a miserable time at Christmas to be fair.

In 2011 Waitrose reported that sales of panettone overtook sales of Christmas cake for the first time. But breathe a sigh of relief – it seems that Waitrose customers are not representative of the rest of the country (funny that). In that year 7 million

Christmas cakes were sold compared to 1.1 million panettoni. And, of course, we need to add to that number all the Christmas cakes diligently baked in households over the country. I think traditionalists can rest easy; at least for the time being.

THE RISE OF SODA BREAD

This quick bread, associated with Ireland today, is leavened not by yeast, but by the chemical raising agent sodium bicarbonate, more commonly known as bicarbonate of soda in the UK, Ireland, Australia and New Zealand, or baking soda in North America. Soda bread is usually made with plain white or wholemeal wheat flour, or other low gluten flours like barley and oatmeal, producing a tender bread with a close texture similar to a British scone.

Its origins, however, are not Irish and it can be traced back to eighteenth-century America when colonists – mainly from Britain, Ireland and the Netherlands – found that potash, a by-product of wood burning, was an excellent instant leavening agent for time-strapped home cooks who wanted to get fresh leavened bread on the table. The active constituent of potash is potassium carbonate, and it is still used to leaven Dutch gingerbread. The switch to sodium bicarbonate came when the process of making it from common salt was developed in the 1790s. Soda bread quickly caught on across the whole of the British Isles, the technique passed on by returning settlers.

But how does it work? Well, sodium bicarbonate is a mildly alkaline chemical with a subtle salty, mineral taste (as is obvious when drinking soda water), and when it reacts with acid, water and a salt are produced along with bubbles of carbon dioxide. In soda bread, the all-important acid is lactic acid, found in cultured buttermilk. In regular high-gluten bread dough, yeast slowly produces carbon dioxide bubbles, and the elastic gluten stretches with the bubbles, making it rise. In low-gluten plain flour, with little stretch or structure, these slowly expanding bubbles quickly pop. When soda bread ingredients are mixed, carbon dioxide bubbles are produced very quickly, so the bread has to be formed and baked before the weak bubbles get a chance to burst.

There is another story concerning the origin of soda bread; that it was made in Britain by accident in the nineteenth century. At this time bread was adulterated with all sorts of white powders by unscrupulous flour manufacturers and bakers, including alum (another carbonate). The story goes that bread was made with sour milk and flour adulterated with alum causing a fizzy chemical reaction. This story, like all the good ones, is entirely untrue.

DOUGHNUTS

'If God didn't want us to eat donuts, he wouldn't have given us hands.' Homer Simpson

Doughnuts get the job done, being a ball of super-refined sugar, flour and fat. They are instant energy, especially when dunked in coffee; indeed, the combination of caffeine and carbs has been fuelling the United States for over a century and is a popular combination here in the United Kingdom too.

Bits of leftover dough have been deep-fried for centuries, but the doughnut came into being in the United States and is derived from *oliebollen* brought over by Dutch immigrants in the early nineteenth century when they made New Amsterdam their new home (it would later become known as New York). These delicious morsels were – and still are – associated with feasts and fairs, but they were only made in very large amounts when the process of doughnut shaping and frying was mechanised in the early twentieth century. This is because doughnut dough is highly enriched and of a high hydration and is therefore very difficult to handle, so these machines were fantastic at making a great number with little mess. To increase productivity, these dough balls were given holes, significantly cutting their cooking time. But the doughnut's popularity only became stratospheric after the First World War, when US soldiers arrived home. During their time in Europe, they had been given doughnuts by the Salvation Army. These doughboys, as they became known, insisted on eating them at home, and the doughnut – cheap to make, easy to eat – quickly became part of the United States' culinary landscape.

If you want to make doughnuts at home, an electric mixer is needed, such is the stickiness of a modern doughnut dough: per 500 grams of strong flour there may be as many as four eggs, 125 grams of softened butter and 150 millilitres of water. Forget making the rings, instead make balls of around 50 grams in weight, prove and pop into hot oil. They are done in under ten minutes. It's important not to overload the pan because doing so drops the temperature of the fat too much and you'll find the dough will begin to absorb oil, making it greasy and heavy. Once cooked on both sides, they are drained and rolled in sugar, then injected with jam or jelly. Curiously, the original jam doughnuts in Britain were always made by filling the dough with jam before frying, which apparently produces a superior doughnut. Doughnuts had caught on in Britain by the mid-nineteenth century, and one place that developed its own unique variety of doughnut was the Isle of Wight. A recipe for them appears in Eliza Acton's 1845 classic *Modern Cookery for Private Families*, and they are a cross between a doughnut and a minced pie: an enriched doughball is flavoured with spices such as cinnamon, mace and cloves and filled with a mixture of dried fruit and candied citrus peel, all fried in lard and coated in sugar. She noted that 'when they are made in large quantities, as they are at certain seasons on the island, they are drained upon very clean straw'.[25]

In recent years the jam doughnut has become a rather taken-for-granted supermarket staple or a bog-standard bakery commodity, but it was given a new lease of life by expert-baker Justin Gellatly, who perfected the art of doughnut making at St John restaurant in London. His were filled with homemade jams and delicious custards, flavoured with caramel or Parma violets. This led to the doughnut suddenly being reborn as an artisan product, and it's nice to see they have reappeared in the shop windows of high-end bakeries and food markets.

The doughnut may have swamped the market with regard to deep-fried doughs, but we mustn't forget the others scattered around Europe: with the glazed and knotted yum-yum of Scotland; poppy-seed-flavoured *pampushky* of Ukraine; the aniseed and sweet-wine laced *rosquilla* of Spain; apricot-filled *sufganiyah* of Israel; and Italian *zeppole* and French *beignets*; the world really is your (deep-fried) oyster.

LEFTOVER BREAD

Stale bread is a gift to the thrifty cook – so many delicious dishes can be made with it. Unfortunately, modern factory bread with its high water content and plastic wrapping means most bread goes mouldy before it turns stale. It's a sad thing that bread is the UK's most wasted food: a shade under 4.5 million tonnes is binned per year, 32 per cent of all bought bread. Why? Perhaps the value of bread has evaporated. In the Second World War it was illegal to waste bread, anything stale was used up; breadcrumbs were a coating for fried food, for stuffings and puddings or bread sauce; slices for *pain perdu* (French toast, aka eggy-bread) and bread and butter pudding. For centuries slices of stale bread were dried into 'sops', which were put into the bowl before the soup was ladled into it (it is from the word 'sop' that we get the word 'soup'). And then there are the examples from other cuisines: *croûtons* in France, *panzanella* (bread salad) and *pappa pomodoro* (bread and tomato soup) from Italy; and the refreshing fermented Eastern European drink *kvass*, to name but a few.

However, none of these are as iconic as *toast*. The wafting smell of freshly made toast combined with the sight of slow-melting butter is in Britain an almost universal comfort. Most toast today is, of course, made from flabby Chorleywood sliced bread, which produces quite depressingly poor soggy, leathery toast. Proper toast requires proper bread; bread that has gone stale. Making toast used to be a way of using up stale bread, and before the popularity of the electric toaster, making it was quite the artform and there are some very detailed descriptions in old cookbooks as to the best way of making it. I end this chapter with flamboyant Victorian chef Alexis Soyer's wonderful, almost romantic method:

Procure a nice square loaf that had been baked one or two days previously, then with a sharp knife cut off the bottom crust evenly, and then as many slices you require, about a quarter of an inch in thickness. Contrive to have a clear fire: place a slice of the bread upon a toasting-fork, about an inch from one of the sides, hold it a minute before the fire, then turn it, hold it another minute, by which time the bread will be thoroughly hot, then begin to move it gradually to and fro until the whole surface has assumed a yellowish-brown colour, then turn it again, toasting the other side in the same manner; lay it then upon a hot plate, have some fresh or salt butter (which must not be too hard, as pressing it upon the toast would make it heavy), spread a piece over ... and cut the toast into four or six pieces. You will then have toast made to perfection.[26]

BISCUITS AND CAKES

There are a few language issues around biscuits and their cousins. In the UK they are – now at least – thin, crisp, sweet or savoury baked goods, usually made with little or no liquid or egg. A large, catch-all term. The catch-all term in the USA is *cookie* (a word from Middle Dutch meaning 'little cakes'). When the British think of a cookie, it is a specific type of biscuit that is both round and chewy, usually containing chocolate chunks. A biscuit in the US is a specific food, essentially a plain, savoury scone mixture made with flour, bicarbonate of soda and buttermilk. However, if a US biscuit is sweetened with sugar and dried fruits, then it is a scone. In Britain, scones can be sweet or savoury. The infamous quip that 'England and America are two countries separated by the same language'* is certainly relevant when ordering in a bakery. As we will see, the boundary between biscuit and cake is extremely blurred, but I think it's true to say that cakes in the modern sense are derived from biscuits and scones.

---

* This quote is often attributed to Winston Churchill, but it originates in the mid-nineteenth century. The first recorded use of it was in Oscar Wilde's *The Canterville Ghost* (1887).

I've never met a biscuit I didn't like: digestive, shortbread, Bourbon, Jammie Dodger. But after peeking into their past, however, I don't think it would necessarily have always been the case. You see, the word biscuit comes from the Latin *panis biscoctus* and it means 'twice-baked bread'. A medieval example of this is the trenchers that people ate from in the grand hall: thick slices of very rough bread, slowly baked again in cooling bread ovens until hard. Another is the hardtack ship's biscuit, originally made from sliced, unleavened bread that was oven-baked up to four times and lasted for years if kept dry. In a bid to make them palatable, they were crumbled into broths and stews. Austere biscuits such as these were slowly improved as technology evolved, with gentler bakes and lighter touches, bringing us rusks and then crunchy crackers.

Sweet biscuits were also twice baked, but the only extant example still familiar to us is Italian *biscotti*; large, biscuity loaves are baked, sliced while still hot and baked again to produce a slender, hard biscuit that's perfect for dipping in strong, bitter coffee. Sugar and fat (usually in the form of butter) were introduced to biscuit mixtures not just because they improve the flavour but because they get in the way of gluten strands, keeping them nice and crisp. Sweet biscuits have always been a snack food, and their usual thinness makes them quick to bake. They are not usually leavened, though a little lift is introduced by whipping butter and sugar, or by adding a pinch of baking powder. Any significant rising is tempered with prick marks – a process called docking – which is almost always present on bought, factory-made biscuits such as digestives, rich tea and shortbread. Most biscuits are baked until very crisp, but some still retain an element of softness or chewiness, the best example of these being oaty flapjacks and American cookies.

Sweet biscuits also went through many changes to arrive at the plethora of types we are familiar with today. In the Middle Ages biscuits called cracknels were very popular. They were sweet but fried, so not a true biscuit, but they then morphed into *croquants*, very crisp and baked. In English recipes dating to the sixteenth and seventeenth centuries, recipes crop up for *biskets*. One recipe for almond biskets appearing in the 1685 edition of Robert May's book *The Accomplisht Cook* instructs that they are made from whisked eggs and sugar, flour and ground almonds, producing something halfway between a biscuit and a cake. At the same time in Scotland, folk were making baked goods called biscuits in the form of large, flat cakes enriched with butter and sugar. Entering the Georgian period, we see biscuits appearing in a form we would regard as modern; however, without our mod-cons, such 'common biscuits', as they were called, were laborious to produce. Take this example from Elizabeth Raffald in 1769, which required a good hour-and-a-half's elbow grease to produce:

TO MAKE COMMON BISCUITS

Beat eight Eggs half an Hour, put in a Pound of Sugar beat and sifted, with the Rind of a Lemon grated, Whisk it an Hour 'till it looks light, then put in a Pound of Flour, with a little Rose Water, and bake them in Tins, or on Papers, with Sugar over them.[1]

Biscuits become more complex in the Victorian era. *Mrs Beeton's Book of Household Management* (1861) has a recipe for 'cocoa-nut' biscuits, which are formed into pyramid shapes before baking.

GINGERBREAD

There is a vast array of gingerbreads made around the world, and I cannot do their great variety any justice here, but it is interesting that these confections, sometimes cake-like, sometimes very hard and brittle biscuits (with a broad spectrum of bakes between these two states) are all ginger*breads*. Funnily enough, none of them could be considered true 'breads', because I find no examples at all of gingerbread being yeast leavened. The original gingerbreads, however, were actually made *from* bread: stale breadcrumbs mixed with honey, ginger and other spices to form thick pastes. One late-fourteenth-century recipe tells us not to use just ginger, but also long pepper and red saunders (powdered sandalwood), and another uses saffron, cinnamon, galangal, nutmeg, mace and cardamom. Thick slabs were made and decorated with heraldic symbols and gilded cloves. It is easy to make, and tastes delicious, not unlike a very spicy and dense treacle tart filling. From the sixteenth century onwards, breadcrumbs were beginning to be replaced with wheat flour. These mixtures were also pressed into wooden moulds, turned out and dried before the fire until hard, and gifted to others. Some were huge – one Russian-made mould produced a gingerbread sculpture weighing in at an impressive sixteen kilograms! Figures were the most popular shape, and perhaps from these shapes came the modern gingerbread men of today. Who knows.

Gingerbread would remain a sweetmeat for the rich until the price of spices dropped to an affordable level from the beginning of the nineteenth century. The gingerbreads were not made with refined sugar or honey but with cheap byproducts of the sugar industry – black treacle and molasses – and it is at this point that a real variety cropped up, with different riffs and adaptations to suit whatever ingredients and cooking equipment were to hand.

Gingerbreads for the masses were cooked in great, unleavened, dense blocks made of ginger, lard, wheat flour or oatmeal and treacle. They were often given to poor children, especially at Christmastime. In Grasmere in the Lake District of England, a famous gingerbread has been made since the mid-nineteenth century to a secret recipe. It has a delicious flavour and texture: spicy and brittle, yet with a slight stickiness. It was called rush-bearers' cake, because it was given to the children of the town who carried the rushes into the local church for a traditional day of prayer, the rushes saving the knees of praying parishioners.

Gingerbread of the biscuit kind was associated with fairs, and was often called 'fairings'. It was considered good luck to buy some, and stallholders gave them out in paper bags as prizes. They were small, round and nubbly – the original ginger nuts. They were also a favourite of the hunting classes, who often kept a bag of them in a jacket pocket, should they need pepping up during a drawn-out chase.

The best of the gingerbreads is parkin, a mixture of oatmeal, wheat flour, golden syrup, treacle, butter, eggs and lots of ginger and other ground spices. It is of the slab variety but is leavened with baking powder nowadays. Its texture is wonderful, crumbly from the oats, yet sticky from the syrups. It began life as tharf cake, a mixture of oatmeal, treacle and lard, rolled out and baked on a hearthstone. These cakes were given out on All Soul's Day on 2 November. Few people observe this day now, but in Yorkshire, parkin is still made at this time of year – three days later, on Guy Fawkes Night.

SHORTBREAD

To many, shortbread is linked with Scotland, and the butter-rich biscuits are a key part of the Hogmanay celebrations, given to any First Footers who might visit after the stroke of midnight. Shortbread is *old*. The great food anthropologist Dorothy Hartley believed it dated as far back as the twelfth century; however, I find no evidence for this, and going by her description of them – a type of rusk made from leftover bread – they do qualify as biscuits in the original, twice-baked sense, but I'm not sure that they qualify as anything even approaching those buttery, crumbly biscuits we know and love today.

Shortbread becomes more recognisable in the seventeenth century, lying somewhere between biscuit and pastry. In some recipes, the dough is leavened with yeast, but by the Victorian era, the yeast has been ditched. Few of these recipes are for a plain shortbread biscuit, they are always flavoured with something, with caraway (a favourite of Mary, Queen of Scots) and candied citron being the most popular. They were opulent in Ayrshire, enriched with egg and cream, and in secluded Shetland they were plainer and cooked on a bakestone or griddle, giving clues to its humbler origins.

Though it is most associated with Scotland, shortbread is just one of a larger tribe of biscuits called shortcakes. The best known is probably the Viennese biscuit, piped into swirls, baked and sandwiched in pairs with a layer of buttercream. Shrewsbury cakes are flavoured with nutmeg, Goosnay cakes with ground cinnamon, and Derbyshire wake cakes with caraway, lemon zest and currants. Finally, Aberffraw cakes, hyper-regional Welsh shortcakes, are baked in the shape of queenie-scallop shells.

The term 'short' pops up a lot in baking with respect to biscuits and pastry. When it comes to the finished product, it essentially means crumbly. This texture is achieved by either adding fat (sometimes called 'shortening') or by using flours with low or no gluten. Uncooked biscuits – and indeed pastry – doughs are described as short too; in this sense it is because they cannot be stretched very much (or at all) without breaking into short pieces. Overworked doughs stop being short – in this case the gluten in the flour has begun to develop, making it stretchy and rubbery, and not something that will produce a nice crumbly biscuit. Therefore, the best way to make shortbread is to press the dough out in a round tin, rather than rolling it out. The dough can then be scored into wedges to make petticoat tails, the centre cut out to prevent the tips shattering and crumbling when later broken apart. Their name comes from 'petticoat tallis', a triangular pattern cut out and used as templates by seamstresses to make the bell-hoop petticoats worn by the likes of Elizabeth I and Mary, Queen of Scots. To make these biscuits even more 'short', the dough is not made by creaming butter and sugar, but by rubbing butter into flour. It is my preferred way too, it's a simple recipe and a matter of proportion: three parts flour to two parts butter, to one part icing or caster sugar. The flour itself is a mixture of two parts plain to one part cornflour. Rub butter into flour, add the sugar and bring together to form a dough (additional liquid is not needed). Press out into a tin, prick with a fork, score your lines and bake at a low heat – a good shortbread should be crisp all of the way through, but pale in colour, and requires a close eye. The best advice I have found when it comes to making this elegantly simple classic comes from F. Marian McNeill: 'only the best materials should be used'.[2]

FLAPJACKS

I don't know about you, but I consider the flapjack as some kind of healthy alternative to other types of cake or biscuit, on the account that it contains plenty of rolled oats. They are nothing of the sort, of course – a flapjack isn't a flapjack unless made with lashings of sugar, golden syrup and butter.

The term flapjack causes a little confusion because in other countries, such as the USA, a flapjack isn't a delicious oaty finger biscuit but a sort of pancake, rather like a drop scone. Indeed, this is how they started life in Britain, the 'flap' meaning to throw and catch, i.e. flip, as one does making pancakes. The earliest use of the word flapjack crops up in the obscure 1609 play *Pericles, Prince of Tyre*, supposedly co-written by Shakespeare: 'we'll have flesh for holidays, fish for fasting-days, and moreo'er puddings and flap-jacks, and thou shalt be welcome.'

The oaty flapjacks we know and love in the UK came in the twentieth century, when a switch was made during or just after the Second World War, when wheat was in precious short supply. Rolled oat mixtures cannot be easily cooked on a griddle and so they were instead transferred to the oven. The earliest written recipe comes from 1957 and is a simple mixture of oats, sugar and margarine – the same combination can be found in mass-produced flapjacks and so-called energy bars today. The best flapjacks are of course homemade. I prefer Demerara sugar and golden syrup in mine. Making them at home means you are in full control of texture too: do you like thin, crisp flapjacks? Or are you like me in going for thick, soft and chewy ones? Whatever texture you prefer, a good tip is to remove the tray *before* they look ready; all of that molten butter and sugar give the impression that things still have a way to go, but upon cooling they solidify greatly. Flapjacks are like steaks, if in doubt they are best *underdone*.

THE NATION'S FAVOURITE BISCUITS

Nothing can beat the flavour and texture of a home-baked biscuit, but I have to admit that they are one of the real successes of factory food, because being reasonably large and flat they are too time and energy consuming to make at home in great numbers. The majority of factory-made biscuits have been designed specifically for mass manufacture. Shortbread is one of the few that buck this trend (though recipes had to be adapted for factories), but digestives, hobnobs, custard creams, Wagon Wheels are industrial creations all.

There have been several polls that have attempted to capture a snapshot of the nation's preferences and behaviours with respect to biscuits, and two things are consistent: we can't get enough digestives, and our favourite brand is McVitie's. In a 2021 Statista poll of favourite biscuits, chocolate digestives came in at number one, then Jaffa Cakes at two, followed by plain digestives, Hobnobs and ginger nuts. A YouGov poll had three of their top five a type of digestive biscuit.

McVitie's created their digestive in 1892. The recipe is a secret one, and has supposedly never changed. They didn't invent the biscuit itself, and the Foods of England Project has found the earliest mention of it in print, in the 19 September 1829 edition of the *Manchester Courier and Lancashire General Advertiser*. It seems that the biscuits are Scottish because the notice reads: 'J. Hutchinson, the original introducer and sole proprietor of Abernethy's celebrated Digestive Biscuits … takes this opportunity of cautioning his friends against imposition.' They are very much peddled as a health product because the wholemeal flour has 'the good property of keeping the body in a regular state', and the bicarbonate of soda neutralises stomach acid;* but let's not forget it is made very palatable with sugar. The advertisement continues to tell us that eating digestives 'supersedes the necessity of having recourse to medicine. Sold genuine, in pound packages, sealed at each end, only at the new Confectionary Establishment, 69, bottom of King-street, Manchester.' Another notice, this time in London's *Morning Post* on 24 February 1836 for 'Buss's Digestive Biscuits' shows us that these biscuits had reached the capital. Buss claims that their biscuits contain 'the greatest amount of farinaceous nutriment that can possibly be concentrated into a biscuit'.

I don't know if anyone buys a digestive for its health benefits; they are simply part of the backdrop of the country's food culture, and they have reached this position possibly because they are not too sweet. Crisp, good dunkers, great with cheese; they're not over-dry or boring – indeed, we have Rich Tea to fill that niche!

We are a nation of biscuit eaters and biscuit dunkers: other European countries enjoy dipping their sweet cakes into alcoholic drinks or coffee, but we dip biscuits in tea, and seemingly we are the sole demographic that indulges in this activity.† Biscuit-dunking has even received academic study;

---

* Despite the fact that there is hardly any bicarb in there, and that what there is reacts during cooking to make carbon dioxide.

† The only exceptions to this rule I can find are the Italian habit of dipped biscotti in strong coffee and North Americans dipping cookies or Oreos in milk, but they are very specific combinations, so not the same in my opinion.

according to the *BBC News* website, the biscuits best able to withstand dunking without collapsing into one's brew are oaty Hobnobs. Shortbread comes in second and digestives third.

TEATIME

The habit of taking tea in the afternoons has its origin in the court of Charles II in the 1660s, after his wife, Catherine of Braganza, arrived in England with a substantial dowry that included two small barrels of tea. Naturally, they showed it off by taking a cup at court, sharing it only with their favourites. Once the sycophantic gentry and aristocracy saw this, they wanted it, if they could afford it. In the opening decades of the eighteenth century, Queen Anne – the last of the Stuart monarchs – took afternoon tea most days, but it doesn't look like she was enjoying any cakes or biscuits with it at the same time. The story goes that they were united in the 1840s by the socialite Anna Maria Rundell, seventh Duchess of Bedford, who had started to feel a few hunger pangs in the afternoon (dinnertime had recently moved from early afternoon to the evening time).* She asked for some bread and butter and cakes to be served up to her at around 3pm. Visiting lady friends copied her, and it caught on. Teatime was born.

---

* This happened for several reasons, but a huge factor was the drop in the price of candles.

Origin stories that are attached to particular individuals are usually complete hogwash, but in this case there are elements of truth: dinnertime *did* move to the evening, creating rumbling tummies, and indeed that *is* why teatime was created. However, it happened much sooner, from the mid-eighteenth century. We don't know who the first person was to do it, but they were very wealthy: sugar and cakes were expensive, as was tea, imported at great expense from China. The drop in prices of these exotics didn't happen overnight, though, so this change of behaviour among the masses was a gradual process. It wouldn't be until the 1820s, when the Indian tea plant was spotted in Assam, that tea would become cheap enough to be very popular. By the 1850s everyone was enjoying teatime in some way or form. The middle classes called this meal 'low tea', because it was served from low side tables as they reclined on couches. The working classes, who had adopted the notion too, had a slightly later 'high tea' after they came home from work. It was 'high' because it was served from high tables (i.e. the kitchen table) and it became the main meal of the day. This difference in eating habits still endures with some folk calling their main meal dinner, others calling it tea. It's the subject of many an argument as to who is using the correct word. But it's not that one is wrong and the other right, it's simply a matter of class.

The treats laid out for teatimes in the eighteenth and majority of the nineteenth centuries were fairly plain, and much less sweet then one might expect, made up of bread, butter, jam, leftover cold meat or fish, simple pound cakes and seed cakes, and perhaps some hot muffins or crumpets. For the middle classes, with something to prove, informal teatimes became, as historian Annie Gray puts it, 'a rule-ridden, etiquette-led ceremony'[3] and a cause of great social anxiety. Those held in country houses would become lavish and large, but the food remained fairly simple (though there was *lots* of it). We had to wait for the very-late-Victorian era before the cucumber finger sandwiches (the smashed avocado on toast of its day) and the expensive patisserie-focused teas served in posh London hotels emerged.

Afternoon-tea breaks also became essential in the workplace, with factory owners filling their workers with sugar and caffeine, the energy boost required to counteract that afternoon lull. Tea and factory-made cakes and biscuits fuelled the workers, who were themselves fuelling the industrial revolution, and by extension, the British Empire. Completing the circle, the Empire imported its exotics – tea, sugar, spices – acquired by slave labour and exploitation of others, to give to the overworked and exploited factory workers to work even harder.

POUND CAKE

The common pound cake is a cake taken for granted, it being the base of many others, and we have probably all made one. It is called a pound cake because equal weights of the four main ingredients – sugar, butter, egg and self-raising flour – add up to one pound in weight. In France this cake is called *quatre-quarts* or 'four quarters' for this reason. It is made by creaming butter and sugar together until pale and fluffy. Eggs are beaten in one by one, until 'accepted' by the mixture; the flour is then carefully folded in – a stage best done by hand. If your mixture curdles as you add your egg, it can be dealt with by adding a tablespoon of the flour and beating the mixture hard, the flour helping to emulsify things. Working the mixture like this does develop the gluten, but because there is just a spoonful of flour, there wouldn't be enough to toughen the sponge. A cake made with curdled batter is perfectly edible, it just won't attain the lift one expects from a good sponge cake. Lastly, a tablespoon or two of milk (or other liquid or flavouring) is added to give the mixture 'dropping consistency', meaning that the mixture easily falls off your spoon with a very gentle tap.

The most important stage is the first: working the butter and sugar together to make sure the butter is extremely soft – but not melted. The best way to achieve this is to leave the butter out of the fridge before you start working it; however, if you forget, weigh your butter, cut into one-centimetre slices and slip them into just-warm water. It will be soft in just a couple of minutes. Old recipes instruct you to beat butter and sugar together by hand for half-an-hour, but now we can use an electric beater. Indeed, if you are in a real rush, the beater can be used to simply – but very briefly – beat all of the ingredients together in the 'all-in-one method', which requires very soft butter indeed to blend everything together without toughening the finished sponge. These cakes have been baked in a variety of tins: round, loaf and fancy copper moulds, but from the twentieth century, they have typically been baked in rectangular loaf tins. It is a wonderful cake if made well and carefully, and it can be flavoured with myriad things: caraway for seed cake, cocoa for chocolate cake, coffee and walnuts, and of course glacé cherries.

We are very much dependent upon chemical raising agents to make modern sponge cakes, but it may surprise you to hear that pound cakes predate them, using instead whisked eggs to give the mixture lift. Sometimes smelling salts were added because they naturally react with the acids in the eggs to produce bubbles of carbon dioxide. The cakes were also originally much larger, and *each ingredient* weighed a pound. Take Hannah Glasse's pound cake recipe published in 1747:

> Take a Pound of Butter, beat it in an earthen Pan, with your Hand one Way, till it is like a fine thick Cream; then have ready twelve Eggs, but half the Whites, beat them well, and beat them up with the Butter, a Pound of Flour beat in it, and a Pound of Sugar, and a few Carraways; beat it all well together for an Hour with your Hand, or a great wooden Spoon. Butter a Pan, and put it in and bake it an Hour in a quick Oven.[4]

Compare this with the mere seconds it can take to make a sponge today and I am sure you'll agree we have never had it so good!

SPONGE CAKES

The basic ingredients of a sponge cake are plain flour, eggs, sugar and (usually) butter; these ingredients can be combined in several different ways to create an array of different sponges. The most important substance to incorporate into a sponge is gas, and it is done in three ways: by creaming butter and sugar together until pale and fluffy, by whisking eggs and sugar, or by including a chemical raising agent with the flour. Sometimes more than one of these methods are used.

The most common method today, the creaming method, is in fact the most recent, and is used to make Victoria sponges as well as the pound cakes described above. All of the other sponges use whisked eggs for aeration, usually stabilised with sugar. Egg whites are high in albumen; long, thin proteins that form webs which trap pockets of air if agitated with a whisk. Sugar helps stabilise the structure, even more so if whisked over a pan of just-simmering water to a temperature of 32 degrees Celsius. The egg is sufficiently whisked when it reaches the 'ribbon stage'. This is when pale ribbons of mixture stream off the tip of the whisk, looking like ribbons as they land, before disappearing after three or four seconds. Now the flour can be folded through the mixture with a metal spoon. This fatless 'simple sponge' is used for a variety of cakes such as Swiss rolls and boudoir biscuits – those crisp sponge fingers covered in a sprinkle of crystallised sugar. They are so named because it was in the boudoir that French ladies ate them in France in the nineteenth century. Here they were dipped in sweet wines, something which obviously caught on because they continue to be dipped in various boozes to make a whole host of desserts such as tiramisu and good old sherry trifle.

More complex is the genoise sponge, which is a simple sponge with a little cooled, melted butter folded through the batter after the flour has been incorporated. I think my personal success rate when it comes to making these sponges is around 75 per cent – folding the flour then the butter requires patience and practice: under-mixing leaves pockets of flour and a greasy layer of butter at the bottom; over-mixing produces a sunken, rubbery cake. One reason this is so tricky is that as soon as butter is added, the butterfat immediately begins to pop the eggy bubbles. A genoise fine cake is even more difficult because double the butter is added. The genoise was created in the nineteenth century in France to mark the successful siege of the city of Genoa, Italy.

Then there are the variations on this theme: for a joconde, a proportion of the flour is replaced with ground nuts; and in a dacquoise all of the flour is replaced with ground nuts – great for those who can't eat gluten, though you could argue it is a type of meringue or macaron, rather than a cake. American angel cakes are the lightest of all, using no fat and just egg whites. The cooked sponges are so light they have to be cooled upside down in their tins to prevent them from collapsing under their own weight.

Perhaps the most revered sponge cakes are scallop-shaped *madeleines*. They are the exact opposite of angel cake: dense and rich with egg yolks and sugar, enriched with brown butter and flavoured with just a suspicion of lemon. These little cakes have to be dense, for they are designed to be dipped into liqueurs. Madeira cake is denser than regular sponge cake for the same reason; designed as it is to be dipped into sweet Madeira wines, hence its name. We have sadly lost the habit.

CAKE CHEMISTRY

'A cake', says Harold McGee, 'is a web of flour, eggs, sugar, and butter … a delicate structure that readily disintegrates in the mouth.'[5] Their structural integrity is created by setting and cooking a batter of starch, gluten and egg protein around countless bubbles of gas in order to produce a melt-in-the-mouth texture. Sugar and fat compromise this lightness, weakening the structure of the baking batter, but introducing richness and flavour. This is true for any sponge cake. Let's have a look at how the ingredients interact with each other in a little more detail.

In order to successfully produce a light sponge, your butter must be very soft. Heed Mrs Beeton's advice: '*Good butter* should always be used in the manufacture of cakes; and if beaten to a cream, it saves much time and labour to warm, but not melt, it before beating.'[6] The paler and fluffier the butter, the more bubbles will form, resulting in a lighter cake. Some cakes use melted butter (e.g. ginger loaf) or vegetable oil (e.g. carrot cake); here the fat cannot trap any air, and we rely entirely on baking powder to produce bubbles. It therefore produces a denser, but moister cake.

Sugar adds both sweetness and richness (especially when in the form of dark brown sugar or golden syrup). Caster sugar also stabilises egg proteins as they capture air in the initial stages of making a genoise, but it destroys as well as it creates, because sugar prevents the formation of bonds between gluten and starch molecules in the flour, introduced last into the cake mix. Just enough sugar makes the cake tender, too much and your batter might collapse. This is one of the reasons why weighing ingredients accurately is so important.

Eggs bind and provide structure to a baking batter. It is really important to use eggs that are at room temperature: adding fridge-cold eggs to well-creamed butter will only cool and solidify it, shearing away the pockets of air you have just spent good time creating. Plain wheat flour is mostly used to make cakes, although especially low gluten 'cake flour' is available. I cannot tell the difference between the two with regard to cake making, and you need a bit of gluten in there anyway – a *little* bit of spring is required. The gluten has to be developed just a tad, and for the best results, it should be gently folded in by hand and with a metal spoon.

The most important element of cake batter is the gas. If using baking powder, bubbles of carbon dioxide form preferentially into the preexisting bubbles suspended in the mixture – hence the importance of the initial creaming stage. As the batter bakes and reaches a temperature of about 60 degrees Celsius, starches begin to gelate, and egg proteins begin to coagulate providing some strength to those thin skins of batter.

The batter has yet to turn solid at this temperature, so as the bubbles expand in the heat, they stretch and thin out the batter. This is why you shouldn't open the oven door when a cake is baking; a drop in temperature shrinks the bubbles, and the cake collapses. At a temperature between 80 and 100 degrees Celsius, starches and proteins coagulate fully, meaning that as the baked cake cools, its structure remains.

But how do you know when your cake is ready? Mrs Beeton provided a timeless tip: 'plunge a clean knife into the middle of it … and if it looks the least bit sticky, put the cake back.' I find a wooden cocktail stick works better, uncooked batter sticks to it readily, helping you tell the difference between uncooked mixture and soft and moist cake. Another way to check is to gently press the cake, if the indentation left springs back, the cake is done. Light sponges also come away from the side of the tin when they are ready, so keep an eagle eye for that important cue. But what about if your cake is all golden brown on top, but is still liquid in the centre? Mrs Beeton has more advice: simply 'put a sheet of clean paper over the top'.[7] It's especially important for anyone baking a cake with a long cook time, like the annual Christmas cake with its mammoth three-hour bake.

TEA LOAVES

Familiar to both the British and Irish tea table, tea loaves are simple to make, at least since the advent of baking powder. Usually denser than regular sponge cakes and often flavoured with dried fruits and dark brown sugar, they are made in loaf shapes and traditionally eaten at teatime. At one time, like bread, they were leavened by the action of yeast. Some still are, and it is very difficult to draw the line between bread and cake in the world of the tea loaf, with most sharing characteristics with both. There are too many of them to discuss them all, so I'm highlighting my personal favourites, going from the most bread-like to the cakiest.

There are some people who, since the adoption of supposedly superior chemical raising agents, think we would find a traditional yeast-leavened tea bread unpalatable. This is complete nonsense because my personal favourite, lardy cake, is one of these. Jane Grigson described them as 'a kind of rural Chelsea bun': an enriched bread dough rolled out and spread with lard, sugar and dried fruit, before being folded, rolled again, only to showered with more fat, fruit and sugar. 'The more lard, sugar and fruit you can cram in the better', wrote Jane; the precise amount of lard needed 'will depend on how much Wiltshire mud runs through your veins'.* They are very calorific, Elizabeth David called them 'a dietician's nightmare'. Only half-joking, she went on: 'Like every packet of cigarettes, every lardy cake should carry a health warning.' It is important to remember that lardy cakes were a seasonal product, made for harvesttime, a point in the year when toiling workers required all of the calories they could get.[8]

---

* The county was excellent pig country, so lardy cake became associated with the place; Grigson (1992) p.310.

Saffron cake, another yeasted cake, used to be made across the country, but has ended up a Cornish speciality, probably because saffron used to be grown in the Cornish town of Stratton. Famously expensive, it was laborious to grow and prepare for market, and there was much adulteration with other, similar yellow-orange dyes. Therefore, it became the done thing to leave the whole strands of saffron in the hot milk from which the colour and flavour were extracted; proof the real stuff had been used. Going all the way back to the mid-seventeenth century, Sir Kenelm Digby's 'Excellent Cake' isn't dissimilar to a modern saffron cake: yeast-leavened, enriched with butter, plenty of dried fruit and a good dose of spice. His was huge, though, requiring 'a Peck of fine flower' (around 6.5 kilograms), 'six pounds of fresh butter' (2.75 kilograms) and 'half a quarter of an Ounce of Saffron', approximately four one-gram jars.[9]

Then there are the dozens of currant tea breads of England, the Welsh *bara brith* and Irish *barm brack*, all of which are now chemically leavened. It was thought (incorrectly, by the English) that the 'barm' in barm brack was a dead giveaway of the cake's yeasty-past (*barm* meaning liquid yeast), but barm brack does in fact translate as 'speckled bread'. You could include the dense, dark and fruity black bun of Hogmanay, a speciality of the Scots and a highly enriched treacly bread covered in white bread dough, which now exists as a fruit cake covered in shortcrust pastry.

Finally, we have banana bread, now forever linked with the first lockdown of the Covid-19 epidemic. Baking this loaf became a viral trend, which acted as distraction to the existential threat of the virus. It was also antidote to those hardcore Instagram bakers who were churning out their sourdough loaves. 'For those who lacked the confidence or fungus required of a sourdough starter', wrote Kaete O'Connell, 'banana bread offered a simple alternative.'[10] And why not? The bananas keep everything moist, guarding the novice baker's mixture from over-baking. Tender and delicious, and mixed in a matter of seconds, it is a wonder of modern baking.

BROWNIES

The chocolate brownie exemplifies all that is great about American baking: generous, rich, indulgent and highly calorific. Just compare UK biscuits with US cookies, UK butterfly buns and Victoria sponges with US muffins and carrot cakes. Brownies are a relative newcomer to the British Isles, and first gained popularity around the year 2000. We have since taken them to our hearts, and they are often enjoyed as either a teatime treat or a dessert. One of the reasons the Brits like a brownie – I believe – is because they are a great example of good stodge: melted butter, real chocolate, lots of cocoa and just enough flour to hold things together – fudgy and squishy. If the brownie had been invented in the UK we'd be calling it a pudding,

The most difficult part of making brownies is judging the cooking time. The 1976 edition of the American classic *Fanny*

Farmer Cookbook warns us: 'Don't overbake: brownies should be moist and chewy.'[11] Brownies must be baked underdone, and removed from the oven when their insides are still on the raw-looking side – they continue to cook outside of the oven and firm up as they cool. If you leave them in until the skewer test tells you they are cooked, what you end up with is a kind of cakey biscuit. Admittedly, it still tastes good, but it is not a brownie. Judging the timing is made all the more difficult because their tops dry and crack a great deal; all part of their charm, but it does make brownie baking a skill in its own right.

Brownies seem to originate in Northwest USA in the late nineteenth century, the earliest recipe popping up in a Sears catalogue of all places in 1897, but it is believed that the first brownie was made in 1893 at the Palmer House Hotel in Chicago, when the chef made an extra luscious, extra thick chocolate cookie, which was cut into bars and glazed with apricot jam. The finger-shaped treats could be eaten more easily, and therefore more daintily, by ladies taking coffee refreshment in the afternoon. These new traybakes took off big time and there was a period of 'brownie frenzy' in the USA from the 1890s to 1920s – something you could argue happened in the UK, but 100 years later. There are lots of recipes in cookery books of the early twentieth century which differ from modern ones in their addition of molasses instead of sugar, and cocoa instead of chocolate. They are now one of the most commonly home-baked cakes in the USA and the number of preparatory mixes available are a testament to this.

ICINGS AND GLAZES

I'm not the most enthusiastic cake decorator, but even I see the importance of a good layer of icing, butter icing or glaze, because aside from looking nice, they introduce decadent textures and, in many cases, protection, whether that be from the elements or from accidental knocks. Growing up in the late 1970s and 80s, when I think of icings, I see buttercreamed butterfly buns and fairy cakes dipped in a simple water icing, covered in desiccated coconut. Topped off perhaps with half a glacé cherry or a diamond of emerald-green angelica. These baked treats are just a vehicle for sugary icing, let's face it.

Simple water icing is used for iced fingers, brushed over Belgian buns and poured over Bakewell tarts.* It is sometimes cut with lemon juice instead of water, and is made by simply beating sifted icing sugar into the water or juice. It's amazing that 125 grams of icing sugar is taken up with just a tablespoon of water to make an icing of spreadable consistency. Much thinner water icing, the consistency of thin paint, is made to glaze ring doughnuts and yum-yums.

More robust icing is made for larger cakes, the classic being marzipan. A lot of people think they don't like marzipan, and if you are one of those people, I think your mind could be changed if you made your own. The shop-bought stuff is just sugar paste flavoured with fake almond essence and dyed a suspicious shade of yellow. Home-made is a more textured mix of ground almonds, and an equal weight of

---

* And ruining them, in my opinion; Mr Kipling has a lot to answer for.

sugar (a combination of icing and caster sugar in a proportion of around 3:1) plus an egg to bind. Mixed and kneaded, it can be rolled and glued to a cake first brushed with a layer of warm, sieved apricot jam. The marzipanned cake then needs a couple of days for it to dry a little, and then royal icing can be spread and piped over the marzipan. My rule of thumb for this kind of icing is to beat 500 grams of icing sugar, a couple of tablespoons at a time, into two lightly whisked egg whites, then loosen slightly with a couple of tablespoons of lemon juice. Spreading neatly is easy with a palette knife dipped in hot water. Professionals go a lot further, building their royal icing in layers: first a thick plaster; then a second, thinner and easier to smooth layer, and then finishing with even thinner, pipeable, decorative icing. Royal icing seems to be on the wane, replaced by the worst of all icings, the often brightly coloured sugar paste (often sold as fondant icing, which it certainly is not), the factory-cake-makers' go-to. Real fondant icing is made by boiling a sugar syrup with a little glucose syrup to the soft ball stage (115 degrees Celsius), and then beating icing sugar into it, and it's best left to the professionals.

The best type of icing has to be the buttercream, of which there are quite a variety, some of which are difficult to make and are all dangerously delicious. A basic buttercream icing can be made by beating unsalted butter until fluffy, and then adding icing sugar to a final ratio of one-part butter to two-parts icing sugar. Little can go wrong; just make sure the butter is suitably softened and pale, because, like a good cake, a good buttercream requires fluffy, aerated butter. Anything fatty can be introduced, hence the very successful inclusion of cream cheese in carrot cakes.* Next up is custard buttercream (*crème au beurre*), made from a very sweet egg-yolk custard which is cooled, strained and whipped into beaten butter. For a *crème au beurre meringue*, a meringue mixture is made over a bowl of simmering water, cooled and then beaten into whipped butter. The most luscious of all is *crème au beurre mousseline*: a sugar syrup is heated in a small saucepan to the soft ball stage, at the same time as egg yolks are beaten until pale and creamy. The hot sugar is beaten into the yolks in a steady, constant stream until cool, and the mixture is then folded into fluffed butter.

The newest icing in the confectioner's arsenal is the mirror glaze. It, and the Russian chef who invented it, Olga Noskova, became a viral sensation in 2016. Her glaze uses white chocolate and can therefore be dyed in any colour. It is made by boiling up a sugar syrup with condensed milk, which is then poured over white chocolate and pre-soaked gelatine leaves. Once these ingredients are incorporated it can be dyed. All sounds good thus far, but here's the rub: the glaze can only be used in a temperature window of 32 to 34 degrees Celsius, and then must be poured over a *frozen* cake. Too much planning and far too sweet for my tastes; give me a simple bun glaze – just boiled sugar and water – painted over a Chelsea or hot cross bun any day of the week.

---

* Carrot cakes are, by the way, much better if made with parsnips.

WEDDING CAKE

The British do love their fruit cakes – or plum cakes as they were once called – and the richest and most dense of these is the traditional wedding cake, wrapped in its double layer of marzipan and royal icing. This cake is eaten at Christmas too, of course, but it's a cake under threat: wedding cakes are getting lighter and fresher. Just think of the lemon and elderflower cake made for Prince Harry and Meghan Markle's wedding. Their density used to be their most important characteristic, because they kept for such a long time and were made of expensive ingredients, and were therefore perfect for a celebration, but now we have refrigerators and freezers and don't have to rely on density to preserve a cake.

Some people say that the marzipanning and icing of the fruit cake was invented out of necessity in the seventeenth century, during the protectorship of Puritan Oliver Crowell who banned (or at least frowned upon) frivolities such as simnel cake, with its marzipan layer, when folk should be focused upon Holy Week and fasting during Lent. The same went for the traditional Twelfth cake made with its coating of icing, eaten on the last day of Christmas. The old misery guts couldn't touch Christmas Day itself, so folk combined the two cakes, creating the Christmas cake. Like all the best stories, it's a false one, and I have to admit falling for it in the past. For starters neither Twelfth cake nor simnel cake existed in those forms in the seventeenth century. No, the wedding cake came first, and the inventor, it seems, was the visionary eighteenth-century cook and entrepreneur

Elizabeth Raffald, her 'Bride Cake' appearing in print for the very first time in her 1769 book *The Experienced English Housekeeper* as an alternative to the traditional 'Bride Pye'. Since its creation, Elizabeth's cake has been made for centuries and the ingredients are just what you would expect: dried fruit, spices, candied citron, almonds. It is made by the creaming method, and air is introduced by the addition of whisked eggs. Her 'Almond Iceing' is made of ground almonds, sugar, egg whites and rose water (an excellent addition). She tells us: 'lay your Iceing on, and put it in [the oven] to Brown.' For her 'Sugar Iceing for the Bride Cake' a classic royal icing is made from whisked egg whites, icing sugar and a little starch to help stabilise it. It is spread straight on top of the hot, set marzipan and allowed to dry out.[12] These cakes were huge and took hours to bake. Elizabeth baked hers in wooden hoops called garths, which heated the cakes gently, baking them more evenly without scorching the outside. Mrs Beeton's advice is that the heat of the oven 'should not be too fierce, but have a good soaking heat'.[13] Perhaps the most infamous wedding cake is the one made for the marriage of Queen Victoria and Prince Albert. It was made at Windsor Castle by the confectioner John Chichester Mawditt. It weighed 136 kilograms and had a circumference of 2.7 metres. It was decorated with a host of sugar cherubs and foot-high models of Britannia blessing the happy couple. But the largest wedding cake ever made was created in 2004 at the Mohegan Sun Hotel and Casino in Connecticut, USA. It weighed 6.8 metric tons, and there is a fantastic photograph of a chef decorating the cake, standing in a cherry picker.

Fruit cakes such as these really do keep. In 2007 an untouched fruit cake still in its original tin was found in Antarctica, left behind from the ill-fated *Terra Nova* expedition of 1910–13. When the tin was opened 'the cake looked and smelled edible.'[14] Cakes such as these keep so well there is no need to feed them with some brandy or rum; every week over the space of a few weeks, 'fed' cakes have a tablespoon or two of the chosen booze trickled on them to make them even richer and to help the cake keep for longer, an activity that doesn't have the history you might think. Research done by historian Annie Gray shows that this 'perplexing habit' crept in during the 1980s, and seems to have been introduced by one Mrs Delia Smith.[15]

These cakes may not be the popular centrepieces they once were, but they have been present at some of our most important celebrations and life events, and the fruit cake's importance to our food culture and identity cannot be overestimated.

SIMNEL CAKE

My personal favourite of all the celebration fruit cakes has to be the Easter simnel cake – it's much lighter than the boozy Christmas cake and has not one, but two marzipan layers (one on the top, the other, baked unctuously into the centre) and no sickly icing. The cake is crowned with a ring of marzipan balls, the precise number of which is hotly debated: 'Since they are said to represent the 12 apostles', wrote historian Laura Mason, 'some contend there should be 11 (thus excluding Judas); others say there should be 13 (to include Christ).'[16] I go with twelve because it makes for symmetrical slicing. This delicious cake is associated with Eastertime, but it was once made specifically for Mothering Sunday, the fourth Sunday of Lent. It has a very long history and has gone through many changes. The familiar form is fairly modern, just popping up at some point in the Edwardian era. In fact, the simnel has only been a cake since the second half of the nineteenth century. Prior to that, it was a strange pasty-cake-pudding hybrid: a fruity, spiced mixture sometimes containing almonds, boiled in a cloth like a Dickensian plum pudding, wrapped in a layer of pastry, baked in the oven and then glazed with egg. A nineteenth-century reminiscence of these simnels was captured in Victorian magazine *Table Talk*: 'The result was so hard and unresisting that one of our country women who received one from some English friends did not suppose it was edible.' It was common for female domestic servants to cook one up and gift it to their mothers on Mothering Sunday. Some say that it is in this form that the simnel cake was first invented and *Table Talk* provides us with a retelling of the origin story: 'Tradition says that a woman called Nellie ... started to make a [batter]. Her husband, Simon, declared it should be boiled, while she insisted that it ought to be baked.' There was fisty-cuffs, but 'a compromise was declared, and it was first boiled and then baked. Hence its name Sim-Nel.'[17] This is, of course, a joke, and the simnel's origins stretch much further back; in the seventeenth century it was a yeast-leavened spiced fruit bread – very expensive to produce at the time. The pastry coat seems to be a Tudor invention.

The simnel has always been made from the most expensive ingredients at the time, which explains why it becomes simpler as we travel back in time, and if we go right back to its origins in the Middle Ages, it was a loaf of bread made from the whitest and highest-quality wheat flour available at the time. The word simnel comes from the Norman *simenel*, which is ultimately derived from the Latin word *similia*, a type of white wheat flour. These early simnels were once ranked alongside fancy manchet bread and only available to the very highest echelons of society. I'm sure you'll agree with me that the simnel cake has been on quite a journey since then!

THE GREAT CREAM-TEA DEBATE

A delicious cream tea, made up of a scone, jam, a good amount of clotted cream and a nice pot of tea is difficult to beat. Both the people of Cornwall and Devon lay claim to being its inventors, the Cornish pooh-poohing the Devonian claim and vice versa. There is an important difference between how the two counties prepare them: for a Cornish cream tea one applies jam first and then clotted cream; in Devon, it's cream first, then jam. Both counties believe that the other's method is the work of heathens. The argument endures because the reasoning behind both arguments seems water-tight: it's jam *then* cream because one always puts cream on top of sweet fruity things, strawberries, fruit pies, etc. The opposing argument says: clotted cream is so thick it does the same job as butter, and it is very difficult to spread it over soft jam, so therefore it's cream *then* jam. I have always rested upon the latter argument. However, after some experimentation at home, I have concluded that both are correct.

Traditionally made clotted cream is very rich, made by evaporating double cream over a very low heat, producing a cream that is high in butterfat and has a butter-like consistency and an appetising pale crust. I made it once by putting a shallow tray of double cream in an oven set to 100 degrees Celsius overnight. This produces a delicious cream with caramel-flavoured skin. It is also quite runny – a similar viscosity to honey – and is best spooned over jam. Modern clotted cream is made entirely differently: it is heated and centrifuged at a high speed, capturing a higher proportion of fat compared to the traditional method, and it therefore forms a much firmer texture when chilled: very difficult to spread over jam. So there you have it: prepare your scone the Devonian way if your clotted cream is shop-bought, or go Cornish if it is traditionally made.

By the way, the 'cream tea' is a surprisingly modern invention, and the earliest printed reference of one appears in a 1932 article in *The Cornishman* newspaper. At this time, scones were not part of a cream tea; instead, Cornish splits were served. These are soft and pillowy enriched bread rolls, and many reckon that the split is superior to the scone in a cream tea. Apparently, the Devonians adopted scones before the Cornish, so we have another situation where the friendly rivalry between the two counties is stoked: the Cornish claim they invented the cream tea because they invented the split, but the Devonians can claim they invented it because they came up with the cream tea we think of today.

LEMON DRIZZLE CAKE

There have been several polls over recent years attempting to ascertain the nation's favourite cakes. I do however have issues with some of the more popular choices. This is not from the point of deliciousness, you understand, but my issues lie with whether or not they are a cake. A survey by the Big Cake Company in 2021 asked folk to choose their favourite cake from a pre-generated list. Included in that list were sticky toffee pudding and the chocolate éclair, neither of which are, in my opinion, cake. However, 40 per cent of those who took part put lemon drizzle cake at the very top of their list. It's also the most popular cake recipe on the BBC Good Food website. It's a great cake for beginners, so there's no surprise in its popularity: delicious and easy to make. That it is soaked in lemon syrup can turn a slightly overbaked sponge into a delectable, delicious treat. That said, things can go wrong, and usually, it is down to an inefficient soaking of said syrup. Paul Hollywood's recipe uses very little syrup, and therefore if you do overbake the cake, it will remain dry. But even if you have plenty of syrup, the cake can still end up dry if it is poured over it in one go, most of it runs around the sponge rather inside it. I heed Sam Bilton's advice in her recipe for lemon and saffron drizzle cake: stab it all over with a cocktail stick and 'slowly pour the … syrup over the cake allowing the cake to drink up the syrup a little at a time'.[18]

I have always assumed that the lemon drizzle cake was a modern one, perhaps invented around the turn of the millennium. However, if one looks to the internet, you will find many websites declaring that the cake was invented by a Jewish baker called Evelyn Rose in 1967. It is, unfortunately, a myth perpetuated. After its apparent origins were purported in a *Guardian* article in 2021, a letter from reader Rev. C. Mary Austin was received saying: 'Sorry, it was around before then! I clearly remember my mother making it in the 50s and early 60s.' So around a decade prior to Ms Rose's recipe. Shockingly, Rev. Austin continued: 'I didn't much care for it at the time – not enough icing on it!'[19] Food historian Glyn Hughes, who went to great pains to prove the true origins of dozens of our most favourite foods, has found the earliest recipe thus far; in the pages of the 1958 edition of the *Good Housekeeping Book*.

Despite its high fat and sugar content, the lemon drizzle cake was singled out for its potential medical and therapeutic qualities. In their parody paper 'The Ambridge Paradox: Cake Consumption and Metabolic Health in a Defined Rural Population' (2017), C. Micheal observed that in the fictional village of Ambridge, home of *The Archers*, the population, despite putting away a vast amount of tea and cake, have an 'extremely low incidence of metabolic disorders such as obesity and Type 2 diabetes'. Micheal hypothesises that this is all due to 'the synergic properties of several biochemical components of cake, especially the phenolic compounds in varieties with a fruit-based element, such as lemon drizzle' and goes on to conclude 'that cake consumption may be a promising therapeutic supplement to prevent and even treat metabolic disorders'.[20] You heard it here first.

CHOCOLATE CAKE

The UK's second favourite cake is chocolate cake – we live, it seems, in a world of chocoholics. When we imagine eating a chocolate cake, our minds immediately go to a land of bittersweet gooiness. All of these indulgent cakes can be traced to one single ancestor: the Sachertorte, invented in the 1830s by pastry chef to German noble Prince von Metternich, Franz Sacher. It is composed of a rich chocolate sponge cake, apricot jam and chocolate ganache. The cake was a revelation at the time, and it became popular the world over. It also ended up in court, or, rather, two wings of the Sacher family ended up there. One wing owned the well-regarded Demel's pastry shop and claimed theirs to be the genuine Sachertorte, the recipe purchased from the grandson of Franz Sacher. However, the Sachers who owned the upmarket Sacher Hotel were also claiming that their cake was the genuine article. Adding to the confusion, the two cakes were slightly different: Demel's was glazed in apricot jam and then covered in the ganache, while the hotel's was split and sandwiched together with jam, before being glazed with ganache. This clash over such a minor difference seems ridiculous, but it does go to show how important it is to make food in a certain way. We know it doesn't really matter, but it does get us rather riled (see also: cream teas). In the end, the hotel won the case, despite Demel's being the closest to the original recipe. To get around this, Demel's announced instead that they sold the 'original' Sachertorte.

Official recipes are secret, but the sponge is made using whisked eggs for lift, melted chocolate and butter are then folded in, then whisked egg whites, before a mixture of flour and cocoa powder are carefully folded in. Some recipes contain ground almonds or almond paste, some don't use cocoa, but all use melted chocolate. It is not a gooey cake, though, in fact some complain that it is rather dry, but this dryness was actually part of its design, and the secret of its success, because the sponges could be baked *en masse* and stored and transported great distances without spoiling. The teashop or hotel receiving the cakes then only had to glaze them with jam and chocolate.

Only in the twentieth century, with its precision cooking equipment and improved methods of producing silky, rich chocolate, did really indulgent cakes crop up, leaving the poor old Sachertorte rather behind. For me, the king of the chocolate cakes is the Black Forest gateau, created sometime in the 1930s. A dessert rather than a cake for teatime, it is built up of layers of kirsch-soaked chocolate sponge and whipped cream, topped with chocolate curls and whole sour cherries. It became popular in the UK in the 1980s, where cheap imitations became the norm, as, sadly, is so often the case.

The infamous 'death by chocolate' cake, or references to it, pop up in the United States in the 1980s, though I cannot see any consensus as to what it actually was: sometimes a chocolate cake with ganache, others a sort-of chocolate-flavoured tiramisu. It settled down to be the cake and ganache combination in the 1990s, and variations of it go by names such as chocolate fudge cake or devil's food cake, the differences between them not particularly distinct. Nor do we care, just as long as the thing is deeply dark, moist, rich and devilishly decadent.

RED VELVET CAKE

This beloved cake of the USA, with its striking aesthetic of deep brick-red sponge and layers of contrasting white frosting, is a relative newcomer to the United Kingdom. The sponge is a chocolate one, made tender by the use of low-gluten flours and the use of oil instead of butter, hence its velvety texture. Recipes for velvet cakes crop up in American cookery books and journals from the 1870s. None of these are red, though. In fact, why velvet cakes ended up being baked so red is a bit of a mystery, and there are three theories as to why so much food colouring is added to a chocolate velvet cake:

1. Acidic cocoa theory. Cocoa powder is naturally acidic, but when mixed with baking soda, the acidity of the batter changes, making the cocoa change to a 'deep mahogany'

colour.* Most cocoa today is made by a process called 'Dutching', which renders it chemically neutral and therefore no colour change occurs. Therefore, red food colouring was added to make up for this. However, if you go on the internet to look at images of velvet cakes made with natural, acidic cocoa powders, you will see a distinct lack of redness. I therefore reject this theory.

2. Great Depression theory: When times were hard in the Great Depression of the early twentieth century, people couldn't afford much cocoa for their chocolate cake, and they came out a rather wan shade of brown. Colour was topped up with the addition of a red food dye. I'm not sure about this one. Wouldn't you add something brown, not red, to make your cake look like a rich chocolate cake?

3. We-need-to-flog-some-food-colouring theory: some cynical folk have decided that a cake which requires so much red food colouring must have been invented by someone trying to sell a lot of food colouring. Call me a cynic, but this is the one I'm going with.

However it happened, the term 'red velvet cake' first appears in print in 1951.

Since its creation the red velvet cake has become part of the Juneteenth celebrations in the US, especially in the state of Texas. For bakers and chefs (both professional and domestic) of African heritage, the dramatic cake has been given a place

---

* Colour changes commonly occur because of bicarbonate of soda. For example, walnuts can turn purple and blueberries green when they are mixed into an American muffin batter made with baking powder.

of honour on dining and side tables. Juneteenth – 19 June 1865 – is an important date in US history, because it was two years after the Emancipation Proclamation, meaning that enslaved Africans were able to claim their freedom. Red foods are served on this day. 'For black folks', says author Nicole Taylor, 'red is symbolic of sacrifice, bloodshed.'[21] A cake, possibly invented by a pedlar of food colouring, has been repurposed as a potent symbol of the country's dark past. The red velvet cake is testament to how quickly new and important traditions can appear just like that and be so meaningful that they feel like they have been around forever.

CAKE OR BISCUIT?: McVITIE'S VS HMRC

We have seen how some baked goods, and the words used to describe them, do not necessarily keep to a single category, and it can be fun arguing about what category a food belongs to. However, this became rather serious when, in 1991, a tribunal was held to determine whether a Jaffa Cake was a biscuit or a cake. It is a national favourite, often appearing in the top five of favourite *biscuit* polls. Why was this important? Well, it came down to VAT, that 20 per cent rate we pay on many goods and services. Her/His Majesty's Revenue and Customs have some rules about baked goods and VAT, and cakes covered in chocolate do not have VAT added to them. Biscuits have no VAT added, unless they *are* covered in chocolate, and then VAT is added to the sale price. That this difference exists seems ridiculous, but that's the British tax system for you. HMRC says, 'there is no generally accepted definition of either cake or biscuit, but the distinction is usually clear in practice', and Jaffa Cakes were zero rated for VAT, but HMRC 'always had misgivings about whether this was correct'.[22] There was an internal review that decided they should be classed as a biscuit. McVitie's, of course, disagreed and argued that Jaffa Cakes are cakes.

Several factors were discussed at the tribunal to determine which category the Jaffa Cake fell into. It was recognised quickly that the word 'cake' in the name was no indication as to whether it was a cake. Method of production was considered: Jaffa Cake bases were made from a batter of butter, flour, eggs and sugar, like a sponge; it was pointed out that biscuits are typically made from stiff doughs that have to be rolled and baked. Also, cakes are soft, and biscuits are brittle and break with a snap. All good arguments. On the other hand, however, Jaffa Cakes are sold as biscuits, and are found on the biscuit aisle in the supermarket, not the cake aisle. They are also the size of biscuits and are presented and eaten as such. In the end the tribunal decided that Jaffa Cakes had more characterises shared with cakes than biscuits, the clincher being that a stale Jaffa Cake goes hard like a cake, unlike a biscuit which would turn soft. Jaffa Cakes could remain zero rated for VAT. If HMRC had won, McVitie's would have received a bill for a hefty £3 million. Sometimes the petty disagreements matter.

PIES AND PUDDINGS

What makes a pie? What are the important, mandatory elements? I think we can all agree, all pies need a filling of some kind, but after that, we quickly wander into grey areas. The filling is most often wrapped in a pastry-lined vessel of some kind, though, as we'll see, the pies of the Middle Ages *were* the vessel – and it is for this very reason that I have combined them with puddings, a food also cooked in a vessel, bowl, mould, tin, etc. Next question: does the pastry have to be double crusted? Is a top-crust-only pie just a stew with some pastry over it, or is it – in your opinion – a pie? What about if there is pastry beneath the filling only? We can agree that's a tart or flan, but are they pies? The people of the Middle Ages lumped pies and tarts into a single group, but most of us would agree that a *quiche Lorraine* is not a pie, until we cover it in pastry and then it is suddenly a good old bacon and egg pie, one of my favourite school dinners as a child. On the subject of French baking, is a terrine a pie? It's cooked in a high-sided tin, the pastry is above and below the filling; it's just a pork pie, isn't it, but French? What's the difference? For starters, there is some gastronomic snobbery – British food is never as good as French. A pastry terrine is revered, yet a pork pie is often treated with suspicion. There are excellent pork, and other, raised pies to be found and baked in the UK, but the difference is, I believe, that in the UK we have come to rely upon supermarkets to produce our food, and the shortcuts they make have led us to a pork pie filled with nitrates, and a filling that is too homogenous. I hope that after reading this chapter, you seek out a recipe for a proper British pork pie, because it is a very different beast to any supermarket offering.

I mentioned a vessel being important, but I may have been hasty because this leaves out the humble pasty. Thinking about this further, is pastry even necessary? Potato-topped shepherd's pie and fish pie are two of our best national foods, and we can't leave those behind. If potato is allowed, can we include lemon meringue pie with its meringue top? In the USA, pizza, at least in the Northwest, is considered a form of pie.

The foods that crop up in this chapter are all part of the spirit of the pie: good, simple, generous food, though some – as you shall see – have been pretty ostentatious in the past.

COFFYNS AND PASTIES

We begin the evolution of pies and pastry where our stories very often start, in the Middle Ages, a time when pastry shells only served one purpose, as a container in which to cook a filling. The pastry itself was not supposed to be eaten. Pies, or pie-like foods, existed in the ancient world, but their pastry was made from flour, water and oil, meaning that they were fairly soft when raw, and fragile when cooked. It was only during the medieval period that hard fats – butter and lard usually – were added, giving the structure necessary to make high-sided raised pies and deep tarts. Because pies often contained several ingredients and were often variable in their contents – the cooks selecting what was most appropriate to the season and event – it is believed that the word 'pie' is a retraction of the word 'magpie', a bird known for collecting a variety of often expensive things, to reflect this. These early pies were called 'coffyns', and while it may seem wasteful to make a food container from flour, it was much cheaper than producing something made of earthenware. It also didn't limit you in the shape or size of the pie you wanted to create. The favourite flour to use was rye because it bakes very hard and is crack-resistant. Coffyns could be double-crusted – i.e. base and walls and lid – or open tarts, the bases blind baked or dried out in cooling beehive bread ovens. These pies were extremely expensive to make: the ingredients were usually meat, dried fruits, spices and often sugar; one had to have a beehive oven, or access to one, which was, as we have already seen, something that was strictly controlled. One also had to have the flour spare to make one. When served at table, tart fillings were spooned into bowls, and pies were cracked open, meat fished out, to a 'mess' of two or four diners: a real social food. After tables were cleared, and without the glare of the guests' beady eyes upon them, servants 'would often gnaw the tough but tasty fragments' which had absorbed some of the cooking juices.[1]

Pastry recipes for these really early pies and tarts sadly do not exist, but methods have been inferred from museum collections, archaeology and clues in texts. There is information about what pies looked like, for example a recipe for a cheese and egg pie in a fourteenth-century manuscript instructs us to 'Make cophyn of þe heghte of þi lyte finger' (Make [the] coffyn the height of the little finger).[2] Another rather fancy recipe for 'Chasletes', or 'little castles', instructs the reader to make several tall, cylindrical coffyns, cut turrets at one end, blind bake them and then fill them with different coloured fillings – yellow, red, white and green – bake again, and just at the point of serving, no doubt with a great fanfare, set alight and carry it into the great hall. Both of these recipes come from fourteenth-century cookery book *Forme of Cury*, written by the master-cooks of King Richard II, so medieval food didn't get fancier.

The other most common British pastry good is the pasty, and I'm sure that if I asked you to imagine one, it would take the form of a Cornish, a cheese and onion, or perhaps even a nice crab pasty, but the first pasties were very different. First of all, they were huge, encasing whole joints of meat such as a leg of wild boar, or a venison haunch. Cooking this way retained all of the juices and flavours, and, most importantly, preserved the meat inside for up to a month. At first, they were made with the rough-and-ready hot water pastry from which coffyns were made, but this was eventually replaced by a more delicate shortcrust pastry. Chunks of meat would also be encased in pastry, often seasoned with spices and covered in butter and suet, but the pasties were still huge and designed to serve several people at dinner. Small pasties did emerge in the Stuart period, but they were fried rather than baked.

Most revered was the venison pasty, the meat eaten only by the highest echelons of society. Butchered joints were wrapped in inch-thick pastry and baked. Then a jug of warmed claret or melted butter was poured through the steam hole, not just enriching the filling inside, but also expelling any air from it, preserving the insides even longer. This way of cooking and preserving meat continued into the early twentieth century for hams. The pastry crust was cracked open, broken down and pressed into the ham's soft fat, then returned to the oven and crisped. A delight now lost to history.

TYPES OF PASTRY

Pies, tarts and some baked puddings require some type of pastry. Many think that making it is difficult, but the vast majority are, in fact, fairly simple to create. Most common are hot water pastry, shortcrust, suet, puff and rough-puff, filo, choux and yeasted pastry (the final two will be dealt with in the patisserie chapter). It can be a little intimidating understanding pastry, but as usual, by looking into its history and evolution, we can feel both enlightened and more enthusiastic about giving it a go.

Let's begin with the word itself. The word *pastry* has the same root as other related foods, *pasta* and *pâté*, as does *paste*; indeed, old recipes, and modern trade manuals, refer to all pastry doughs as pastes. Pâté seems odd here, but pounded meat fillings were baked in a pastry shell, the pastry eventually swapped for an earthenware terrine, but the word *pâté* stuck. Therefore, at one time French pâtés and British pies were equivalent foods.

The secret to making a good pastry is to produce a dough without developing the gluten. Most pastry recipes ask you to rub some fat into flour until the mixture resembles fine breadcrumbs. This stage is important because it means that when the dough is formed, each flour grain with be coated with some fat, all held together with just enough water to make a stiff, pliable dough. The most basic is a mixture of rubbed-in fat and flour, hot water and melted lard, producing a waxy dough called huff paste. It wasn't eaten, but by 1595, some pastes certainly were. In one recipe for a 'fine paste', wheat flour is mixed with the 'yolks of eggs with sweet [fresh] butter, melted', it also says 'you may put [in] saffron and sugar'.[3] No one would be using these very expensive ingredients unless they were eating the final product.

Delicate shortcrust pastry developed at around the same time. Here, all of the fat is rubbed into the flour, moistened and brought to a stiff dough with water. Recipes are variable, but by the mid-eighteenth century, we have largely settled on the modern ratio of half fat to flour, and half sugar to fat for sweet shortcrust. Some of the water is replaced by whole egg or egg yolk, and Sarah Harrison's shortcrust recipe for 'Paste Royal' from 1751 is enriched with cream and sherry. To avoid developing the gluten in the pastry dough, it is best to work quickly and lightly. Eliza Acton told us in 1845: 'The more expeditiously the finer kinds of paste are made and dispatched to the oven, and the less they are touched the better.[4]

Laminated puff and rough-puff pastry are made of layers of dough and butter that are built up by a process of rolling and folding. For puff pastry, a dough is rolled, a slab of very cool butter is hammered out to the same size as the dough, folded over into thirds, turned and rolled six times, producing a dough with 729 layers of butter and dough. For rough-puff paste, butter is either grated or diced before being folded and rolled into the paste. The rolling flattens the pieces of fat, but because the layers of butter are not continuous, the pastry is merely flaky. The first known recipe is in Thomas Dawson's *The Good Huswifes Jewel* (1596) where he instructs the reader to make a dough, roll it out and then 'dot with butter one piece by another, and fold up your paste upon the butter and drive it out again. And do so five or six times.'[5] To achieve a good result, everything must be kept very cold, otherwise layers merge and butter oozes out from any cut sides. In many houses from the Tudor period, there was often a 'pastry', a special room built especially for pastry work, away from the heat of the kitchen and on the north side of the building – the side receiving the least amount of sun – so that it would be as cool as possible.

The doughs of puff pastes are stretched and worked many times, so for these types, gluten development is required – we wouldn't want the dough to break apart, it would ruin the lamination. The baked pastry is not tough because the gluten is being developed in only one plane, and the cooked pastry dough is so thin and crisp it doesn't feel tough. The wonderful rise that is achieved during baking is created from air trapped in the sheets during the folding process and the water found in butter, turning to steam and separating the layers. Puff pastries contain equal amounts of flour and butter, and they are labour-intensive and inefficient to make in small batches. I therefore highly recommend buying it, but do make sure it is of quality and made with real butter, and not some nasty hydrogenated palm oils. Good pastry needs good ingredients.

MINCE PIES

Mince pies are confusing to anyone who isn't British; they are full of 'mincemeat', yet they contain no minced meat – or any meat at all, for that matter. They used to, though, and these meaty mince pies are not as weird as they might sound. They have been eaten since the Middle Ages, when they were filled with the most expensive and exotic ingredients: plenty of meat, dried fruit, spices and sometimes alcohol. These pies, like much of the upper-class food of the Middle Ages, were influenced by the food of the Middle East and North Africa – there's little difference between these pies and a tagine, for example. Mince pies such as these were cracked open at fancy feasts all year round, not just Christmastime.

Cookery books written in the era of the Stuarts provide us with many recipes for 'minc'd pyes'. Robert May's

The Accomplisht Cook (1660) is one of those. The meat used is highly variable; you can choose from lamb or mutton, ox tongue or veal. There are mince pies made for fasting days made with carp, salmon, even sturgeon, and there is one recipe where hard-boiled eggs are used in place of meat. Importantly, May's book doesn't just give us recipes for fillings, but illustrations of what the pies looked like. Some were made into intricate shapes which, when laid out, formed a symmetrical pattern of pies similar to that of a Tudor garden, others were cylindrical and cube-shaped. Around the same time as May's book was published, the Puritans, headed by Lord Protector Oliver Cromwell, identified these indulgent pies as Catholic and tried to stop them from being made at Christmastime.

By the eighteenth century, mincemeat fillings were exactly how we might expect them, with the inclusion of brandy, apples and dark-brown sugar. There was meat – the favourite by far being ox tongue – and suet, the crumbly fat found around the kidneys of a mammal, usually beef, but sometimes veal or mutton. They were still expensive to make, but costs had dropped enough for the middle classes to be able to enjoy them. Some writers noticed too that people needed to economise (keeping up with the Joneses was expensive, after all!) and came up with cheaper recipes, using the chopped meat extracted from boiled calves' feet and even tripe. There are recipes too for mincemeat containing no meat (though plenty of suet), indicating perhaps that people were shifting away from the tagine-like pies towards sweeter, boozier ones. Then, in the Victorian era, the amount of meat really began to fall and there was much more sugar. Many were still expensive to make; Charles Elmé Francatelli's recipe for 'mincemeat a la Royale' (he was Queen Victoria's chef) contained all of the ingredients you might expect plus roast sirloin of beef, 'a proportionate weight of poached pears and preserved ginger' and a triple threat of Christmas booze: brandy, rum and port. Amounts were vast: Alexis Soyer (a man often reckoned to be the first *bona fide* celebrity chef) has one recipe that used, among other things, 640 pounds of dried fruit, 200 pounds of sugar, 350 pounds of suet and 72 bottles of brandy.

In the first edition of *Mrs Beeton's Book of Household Management* there are only two mincemeat recipes. Her standard mincemeat has a small proportion of 'lean beef', and her 'excellent mincemeat' has none at all. Taking a look at her recipes, we see the instruction 'mince the beef and suet', but also to 'pare, core and mince the apples; mince [the] lemon peel'.[6] This does not mean that one had to pass all of these items through a mincing machine: they had yet to be invented. The term 'mincing' meant, until very recently, to chop well, so if you want to accurately recreate some historical or traditional mince pie fillings, you should be chopping all of your ingredients. Beeton's mince pies were now 'patty pan' sized, i.e. small and bitesized.

Modern mass-produced mince pies are very sweet compared to their ancestors, but you will find the old recipes really are the best, and I heartily recommend making meaty mince pies, their deliciousness and succulence cannot be bettered.

BANQUETING PIES

Pies made for large feasts and other special events could be truly astonishing. We have seen the castles made in pastry, but, for me, the best are the fancy raised pies of swan, peacock, pheasant and the like. Seventeenth-century still life paintings 'depict beautifully constructed pastry cases, often decorated with gilded geometric strap-work or acanthus-inspired motifs. They are frequently surmounted with the actual heads, tails and wings of peacocks, swans, pheasants and other birds.' Not only that, but often the plumage and beak were gilded too: around some birds' necks were 'precious-looking golden necklaces'.[7]

Pies were theatre. Seventeenth-century master cook Robert May manages to combine a traditional pie – the bride pie – with some fantastical elements in his instructions on how 'To make an extraordinary Pie, or a Bride Pye of several Compounds, being several distinct pies on one bottom'. The pie is built up like an Aztec temple, but instead of a square base, the base takes the shape of a large flower. It was traditional to break the pie over the bride's head for good luck. It must have been a messy affair at a wedding Robert May catered for, because inside his were 'cock-stones' (cockerels' testicles), veal sweetbreads, ox pallets, oysters, dates, pine kernels, nutmeg, mace and butter. Then, a caudle of white wine or claret and lemon juice was poured into it before serving. May says the pie can be of 'several Compounds', meaning it is just one of group: there would also be an oyster and bone marrow pie, a bird pie stuffed with larks which have been generously stuffed, an artichoke pie and several smaller egg pies.

His most theatrical pie element would sit in the centre of all the others. He tells us: 'you may bake the middle one full of flour, it being bak't and cold, take out the flour in the bottom, and put in live birds or a snake which will seem strange to the beholders.'[8] A pie of four-and-twenty live blackbirds was not just an invention for nursery rhymes.

Pies such as these don't exist anymore: too expensive and they usually contain protected species, or, in the case of the bride pie, have been superseded by the wedding cake – much more civilised and much less messy. I once attempted a three-tier raised wedding pie for a friend's wedding. There was no taxidermy or gilding involved, but it still took me five days to construct and bake, providing me with just an inkling of the work that was required of the master pastry cooks to make such spectacles.

YORKSHIRE CHRISTMAS PYES

Let's take a moment to consider the feasting pie to beat all others, the Yorkshire Christmas pye, a humungous creation, teeming with game and other meats. The huge pies were sent as gifts from Yorkshire landowners with plenty of land and plenty of game living on that land. They would be sent to friends residing in the cities, so they would have to travel quite a distance by horse and carriage. They were traditionally eaten on the Feast of Stephen, 26 December. Chef to Queen Victoria, Charles Elmé Francatelli wrote of them: 'Their substantial aspect renders them worthy of appearing on the side-table of those wealthy epicures who are want to keep up the good old English style, as this season of hospitality and good cheer.'[9]

The first recipe to appear in print pops up in Hannah Glasse's *The Art of Cookery Made Plain and Easy* (1747). She instructs us first to 'make a good Standing Crust, the Wall and Bottom be very thick; bone a Turkey, a Goose, a Fowl, a Partridge, and a Pigeon, season them all very well.' Next, we must '[o]pen the Fowls all down the Back and bone them … lay them in the Crust, so as it will look only like a whole Turky [sic]; then have a Hare ready cased [and] jointed; season it, and lay it as close as you on one Side; on the other Side Woodcock, more Game, and what sort of wild Fowl you can get … put at least four Pounds of Butter into the Pye, then lay on your Lid … and let it be well baked. It must have a very hot oven, and will take at least four Hours.'[10] As you will soon see, this pie was a rather modest one. When it came to eating it, the crust was cracked open, the animals extracted and carved, before being eaten with the spiced butter and jellied juices. The pastry for the pie required a bushel of flour, around 27 kilograms. I was once asked to recreate Hannah's pie for a television programme, and it was a complete disaster. The pie – which took me five days to construct – collapsed within minutes of entering the oven, slumping onto the glass door, spewing melted butter everywhere. What I didn't know at the time was that a strip of metal would have been fastened around the pie, acting like a corset. Later, large, sculptural pie moulds were made from tinned copper to do this job most effectively and decoratively.

An illustration exists of one of Queen Victoria's Christmas pyes. It's being carried into the dining room, and is so big, four footmen are acting as pallbearers. Her chef's recipe included four turkeys, a goose, two pheasants, four partridges, four woodcocks, twelve snipes, four grouse, four widgeons, a Yorkshire ham and two ox tongues. All of the birds were filled with a rich stuffing and French truffles. The cooked pie was then filled with aspic jelly.

However, the largest example of a Christmas pie so far unearthed was found by historian Ivan Day and comes from a grand house in the Lowther Valley in the Lake District, 1763. It contained:

2 Geese, 4 Tame Ducks, 2 Turkeys, 4 Fowls, 1 Wild Goose, 6 Wild Ducks, 3 Teals, 2 Starlings, 12 Partridges, 15 Woodcocks, 2 Guinea Cocks, 3 Snipes, 6 Plovers, 3 Water Hens, 6 Widgeons, 1 Curlew, 46 Yellow Hammers, 15 Sparrows, 2 Chaffinches, 2 Larks, 3 Thrushes, 1 Fieldfare, 6 Pigeons, 4 Blackbirds, 20 Rabbits, 1 Leg of Veal, Half a Ham, 3 Bushels of Flower, 2 Stone of Butter – the Pye weighed 22 stone.

That's 140 kilograms. As Day quips, 'I don't suppose much bird song was heard in the Lowther Valley for some months.'[11]

STRANGE PIES

The British Isles has been home to some weird and wonderful, unique and eccentric pies. There are so many to choose from, a book could be written on this subject alone. Many of them are gastronomically challenging. Historical foods can seem weird or disgusting to us today, and I usually leap to their defence: the recipes in the vast majority of old cookery books are included because people made and enjoyed them. But that's the food of the middle classes and above; for the working-class majority a lot of dishes were created because of a lack of food, or a lack of variety. At best their pies are examples of extreme thriftiness, but many foods of the working classes are born of poverty. Here is a selection to hopefully pique your interest. We'll begin with a fun one.

The Bedfordshire clanger is a kind of pasty made from suet pastry, and what is unusual about it is that it provides the eater with both main course and dessert, because it is a pasty of two halves: one savoury and the other sweet, the favourites being pork or bacon alongside apple, the two separated by a piece of pastry. It's a regional food that has never really travelled out of its county, which, I think, is a shame. It's been made for at least two centuries, serving as an excellent portable food for farm labourers, the filling changing depending upon the home's economy. In its original form it was a boiled roly-poly with a meaty filling and dried fruit mixed into the pastry. The move to baking came in the twentieth century, when folk moved from cooking on open fires or coal ranges to gas cookers. It's nice to see the suet pastry was retained, a pastry often ignored outside of the steamer.

An infamous pie of Southwest England, the stargazy pie is beautiful to behold: a round pie, usually baked on a pie plate, is filled with pilchards or herrings that have been gutted and deboned, but with their heads still on, all arranged like spokes in a wheel, the crust laid over with their little heads poking out of the edges, looking up to the sky. The pie doesn't look like this for aesthetic purposes only, it has a function: as the heads bake in the oven, they release their oil – omega-3, very important – into the filling. The arrangement of fish made it a great communal sharing pie, as historian Dorothy Hartley pointed out, because one can 'divide it into slices with great exactitude'.[12]

Everyone has heard the idiom 'to eat humble pie', used when someone has been cocky with hubris only to find themselves socially embarrassed. Did such a pie exist in real life, though? It is believed that it comes from *umble* (or sometimes *noumbles*) pie. The umbles being the offal of an animal, usually a deer. In the Middle Ages, when a deer was brought back from a hunt, its carcass would be divided, the best part – the loin – going to the man who dealt the killing blow or shot, while the umbles, cooked in a coffyn and eaten as a stew, was served to the lowliest members of the hunting party. To receive it meant you were socially inferior, and therefore begat the saying. The seventeenth-century diarist Samuel Pepys wrote how he, a guest at another's home, ate the 'meanest dinner of beef, shoulder and umbles of venison'.[13]

Sticking with the offal theme, a pie once made by dairy or cattle farmers was muggety pie, made from the umbilical cord of a newly born calf. It was cut into short pieces and then split lengthways, before being simmered for hours until very soft and gelatinous. The pieces were arranged in a pie dish, seasoned and filled with a mixture of the cooking liquor and milk. It was baked and left until cold so that the filling could set to a still jelly before it was eaten.

CORNISH PASTIES

The Cornish pasty is probably Cornwall's most famous food. It's a simple affair, containing beef skirt, potato, swede and onion. The filling is seasoned very well with black pepper and baked in shortcrust pastry made with both lard and butter, and that's it. Don't be tempted to add anything else; giving a Cornish person a pasty containing carrot is a surefire way to cause offense.

There's a romantic origin story for the Cornish pasty which goes something like this: they were given to Cornish tin miners or fieldworkers so they could slip one into their pockets and eat them for lunch, the thick crimp being a useful handle protecting the main meal from dirty fingers – something doubly important for the miners because of the amount of arsenic found within the tin mines. Food historian Glyn Hugues courted controversy in 2020 when he appeared on BBC television and told the nation that while Cornish pasties are certainly associated with the miners, there is no evidence that this is true. There are early photographs dating from the nineteenth century showing the miners eating their pasties, and they are all being eaten from bags – much better at protecting the pasties from damage and arsenic-dusted fingers. He then went a step further, saying that the Cornish didn't even invent them, and that 'people have folded pastry over fillings for 2,000 years'. The headline in the *Sun* newspaper ran: 'ARRR YOU MAD? Historian sparks uproar by claiming the pasty was NOT invented in Cornwall'.[14] Apologies to any Cornish folk reading, but I think he is correct: mixtures of potato, onion and some kind of protein (beef and cheese are the most common) wrapped or covered in pastry have been eaten right across the whole country for centuries now.

If you've never made a pasty in your life, this is the one to start with; all of the ingredients are raw so there is no messy gravy getting everywhere and making things difficult. Amounts of each ingredient are purely to your own taste and budget. It seems too simple to be delicious, but the secret is in the seasoning. Use little or no salt, and you will have a bland stodge-fest before you, and a really good grating of pepper is essential: add what you think is plenty, then do two more turns of the pepper mill. You won't be sorry.

APPLE PIE

Apple pies come in myriad forms and are humble stalwarts of many countries' cuisines. In the UK we have several types and styles, using a variety of flavours and pastries; France has its *tarte aux pommes*, the sweet pastry beneath, apples thinly sliced and beautifully arranged on top. There is *tarte tatin* too: wedges of apple coated in butter and sugar in a heavy pan, top covered with puff pastry, before being slid into the oven, an upside-down pie of excellence. Austria and Germany have their crisp and golden *apfelstruedel*. Apple pie is one, if not *the* national dish of the USA, traditionally baked in a double crust.

Historically speaking, British apple pies are single-layered, and go back to the seventeenth century. What is very obvious from looking at British recipes is that we like our apple pie fillings tart. In the seventeenth century, sour apples, called codlings, were a favourite: they were cooked gently until tender, and a syrup was made from cores and peel, sugar and the juice of sour grapes or crab apples. Sometimes quinces were added for flavour and colour, turning a lovely ruby red when cooked.

From the nineteenth century, we have used the Bramley's Seedling, a tart cooking apple that easily cooks down to a purée. Not everyone's a fan; Elizabeth David complained that they are too sour and collapse down too readily. I believe Ms David is in the minority. I find that cooking two apple varieties is the way to go: Bramley's for the tartness and sauce, and another that won't break down, and is a little sweeter, say a Cox's Orange Pippin or a Russet. I add just enough sugar to take the edge off the tartness, preferring to add a contrasting sweet element in the form of custard or Chantilly cream. I always add a knob of butter to my filling too, as well as a little orange zest, a few sultanas, a pinch of mixed spice and a couple of twists of the pepper mill.

Apples can be baked in desserts in several other ways: they are great peeled and cored, filled with butter and sugar, wrapped in pastry (suet is best) and baked for apple dumplings. Apple Charlotte is made by lining a Pyrex bowl or soufflé dish with buttered stale bread, filling it with apple, making a lid from more buttery bread and baking. Best served with thick cream. My highest recommendation is a rather forgotten regional quirk of Yorkshire, and that is to eat your apple pie with a slice of cheese on it as though the pie slice is a cracker. Don't knock it 'till you've tried it.

CUSTARD TARTS

If, before I popped my clogs, I were given the chance to select a final meal, I would order a very large, artisanal custard tart. It is my favourite food. Even the bad ones – those small ones in foil containers with sloping sides, fluted pastry rims, overcooked custard and soggy, underbaked pastry – are good in my book. A 'proper' homemade custard tart is usually made in a shallow, straight-sided tin, the pastry base, a sweet shortcrust, is baked blind, the custard made from cream and eggs and flavoured with vanilla. Lastly, before it's slid into the oven, a whole freshly grated nutmeg is scattered over the top.

Every cookery book you look in there is a slightly different way of making the custard: is only cream used, or a mixture of milk and cream? Are the eggs whole, or are yolks used, or just the whites? There is a science to what is going on that provides us with a good rule of thumb. For something like a quiche (a savoury custard tart), which requires a firm custard, one egg per 250 millilitres of liquid sets well. If you want a delicate, soft and velvety set, use five medium egg yolks per 250 millilitres. In a baked custard, the eggs thicken and form a gel at around 80 degrees Celsius. This is why you should never allow custard to boil, because over this temperature, the network of solids that form the gel tighten up, making scrambled egg. When you come to bake a custard tart, a low temperature of 120 degrees Celsius will produce a good, even set. It can be an impatient wait: tarts can sit in the oven, seemingly refusing to set, and then suddenly, within the space of a minute or two, the liquid turns that perfect, enticing wobble. A firm tart is an overcooked tart.

Chef Marcus Wareing made the ultimate custard tart as part of a banquet to celebrate the 80th birthday of Queen Elizabeth II in 2006. For his custard he used egg yolks and whipping cream. One issue with baking a larger custard tart is that the inside can still be liquid when the outer rim has already set. He got around this by heating the custard first so that it was already well on its way to setting temperature when it was slid into the oven. When it is ready, he says, 'it should have a slight, even quiver across the top when you gently shake [it].'

The custard tart's links with royalty go back centuries. *Croustades* appear in medieval cookery books, and the food in them was served at royal courts, but it was the name given to the pastry case, not the filling, and they were not necessarily filled with custard. They were usually egg or cream based, though (the English have had a love affair with anything custardy that seemingly goes back to the year dot), and so the name followed the filling. Fillings sat somewhere between sweet and savoury, containing meat like pork, or fish such as salmon, plus dried fruit and small amounts of sugar.

Very sweet custard tarts were called *doucets*, which were round in shape. One was made as part of the dessert course for the coronation feast of Henry IV in 1399 which was flavoured with honey and saffron. There were also very small, deep and round ones called *darioles*, the direct descendants of these being the sloping-sided custard tarts you find in the supermarket today. Vanilla and nutmeg are the standard spices, but before vanilla was commonplace the favourite aromatics were bay leaves, cinnamon, mace and rose or orange flower water. They are worth trying, and I heartily recommend the combination of orange flower water and mace.

A CAUDLE COMEBACK?

Between the sixteenth and eighteenth centuries, the British made their fruit pies in a way we don't anymore, a way to which, I believe, we should return, and that is with the addition of a caudle, a type of custard made of cream, sugar and eggs. Sometimes sweet wine or verjuice – the juice of crab apples or unripe green grapes – were added to make a sort of wine curd. The caudle was added at the end of cooking, often through the central piehole, which was sometimes shaped like a crown to act as a funnel, before the pie was slid back into the oven to set. The result is delicious, the caudle mixing with the cooking juices inside the pie.

Caudles began life as a sort of thin gruel sweetened with sugar or honey and thickened with starch and egg yolks, a dish for the sickroom. But the notion of making them very sweet and rich and adding them to pies and tarts suddenly popped up and then disappeared. I first came across them in Jane Grigson's *English Food*, where she provides a recipe for a raspberry pie that has a caudle of egg yolks, cream and sugar poured into it. Years later, as a chef, I cooked the first known recipe for pumpkin pie from *The Compleat Cook*, written by the mysterious W. M. in 1658. It was quite the thing: thinly sliced pumpkin flesh mixed with the herbs thyme, rosemary, parsley and marjoram, plus cinnamon, nutmeg, black pepper and cloves. These were put into a small frying pan and covered with a sweet egg mixture. This was cooked gently until this bizarre frittata – called a *froize* – was set. Then W. M. tells us to 'fill your Pye, take sliced Apples thinne round wayes, and lay a row of the Froiz, and a layer of Apples with Currans betwixt the layer while your Pye is fitted, and put in a good deal of sweet butter before you close it'. When baked 'take six yolks of Eggs, some white-wine or Verjuyce, & make a Caudle of this, but not too thick; cut up the Lid and put it in … and so serve it up'.[15]

It wasn't just fruit pies that received a caudle. An eighteenth-century cookery writer called, rather pleasingly, Ann Cook gives a recipe for 'Sweet Turbot Pye' that is finished with a caudle of butter, sugar and white wine. But perhaps more enticing is her absolutely divine 'Apple Custard Pye', which involves baking an apple pie, carefully removing its lid and pouring over it a custardy caudle. It's set in the oven, and when ready, the pastry lid is dusted liberally with icing sugar, cut into triangles and arranged neatly atop the pie.

Now caudles are no more, though they did live on a little longer in the county of Cornwall, where caudle chicken pie was enjoyed. It sounds pretty good; an onion and chicken pie is baked and when ready, a savoury mixture of sour cream and eggs is poured through the piehole, and allowed to set. There's nothing I don't like about this. It is obvious to me – and I hope to you too, now – that the caudle is overdue a comeback. Now, who's with me?

JAM TARTS

My introduction to baking was making jam tarts with pastry trimmings with my mum on rainy afternoons in the school holidays, so they hold a special place in my heart. These little, simple tarts have an interesting history, and once took pride of place in the dessert courses of the upper classes.

The furthest I can trace them – or something like them – is in a collection of manuscripts called *Two Fifteenth-Century Cookery-Books*, where within its pages is a recipe for a 'Tarte de ffruyte', made with dried figs cooked in a sweet wine, spiced and further sweetened with raisins. The 'recipe' does give us some information about how the tart looked, because it tells us to 'make faire lowe coffyns'.[16] This filling evolved over the next century or so to become 'tart stuff', a sweet fruity filling for tarts. Most popular was 'black tart stuff' made from wine, prunes and other dried stone fruit. The ingredients were cooked down to a 'thick, rich, gloriously dark prune jam'.[17] Red tart stuff was made of crab apples, yellow stuff from apricots, and green stuff from gooseberries or spinach. They were made with beautiful pastry lattices covering them, some cut into the shape of delicate snowflakes. The lids were made of puff paste and baked separately, dusted with icing sugar and then laid atop the baked tart.

Robert May made what I think were the first true jam tarts, combining elements of the tarts described above into an altogether unique offering, all the way back in 1660. He called them 'Laid Tarts', which were composed of very shallow pastry cases made into some beautiful shapes, with a pattern inside made up of raised pastry strips. The gaps were filled with coloured jams and conserves, creating beautiful tarts that looked like resplendent stained-glass windows, which historian Ivan Day calls 'some of them the most colourful baked goods in the history of English food!'[18]

TREACLE TART

'Here we are children! Come and get your lollipops! Lollipops! Come along my little ones. They're all free today! Cherry pie, cream puffs, ice cream, treacle tart!'

The calls of *Chitty Chitty Bang Bang*'s terrifying Child Catcher still send a shiver down my spine. It is interesting that he uses sugary delicacies to lure children into his cage, he knows they simply cannot resist them. On his list is treacle tart, toothachingly sweet, and a favourite of mine today.

The word treacle is a confusing one – you may instantly think of black treacle – but it is not usually the main ingredient in treacle tart, if it is included at all. Golden syrup is the 'treacle' you are after. Treacle is actually a catch-all term for any of the uncrystallisable sugary syrups left over from refining sugar from sugarcane juice, and it can be a whole range of shades, from a pale straw colour to very dark, almost black molasses. The two available in Britain are golden syrup and black treacle. Mrs Beeton said that treacle 'is of great use as an article of domestic cookery', continuing, 'children are especially fond of it; and it is accounted wholesome.'[19] This is not an opinion healthcare professionals hold today. However, an article from the *Manchester Guardian* from September 1935 tells us that at the time, the British Medical Association was recommending treacle tart as a dessert choice for a mid-week 'high tea'. Before his fateful Antarctic trek, explorer Captain Scott wrote to the Lyle family, the producers of golden syrup: 'Your Golden Syrup has been in daily use in this hut throughout the winter, and has been much appreciated by all members of the expedition.'

Needless to say, Lyle's Golden Syrup was, and still is, an iconic ingredient. The gloopy, butterscotch-tasting syrup, being a byproduct, was sold very cheaply to Lyle's workforce, but news soon got out about just how delicious it was, and Lyle's put it on sale in 1883, and there it has been ever since. They have never changed the design of the tin, except for the weight switching from pounds to grams. Despite its longevity, many people haven't noticed that the logo is made of a dead lion surrounded by bees, with the legend 'Out of the strong came sweetness'. It is, in fact, a biblical reference, from the book of Judges in the Old Testament: Sampson (of haircut fame) is attacked by a lion and defeats it by ripping the creature open. Upon its demise, bees take up home in the carcass, producing fistfuls of honey for Sampson to take back to his family. As the family would want to know from whence it came, he provided them with the riddle: 'And he said unto them, Out of the eater came forth meat, and out of the strong came forth sweetness. And they could not in three days expound the riddle.' Judges 14:14.

Treacle tart, a shortcrust pastry base filled with around two-parts golden syrup to one of stale breadcrumbs, has been made since the 1880s, and so seems to predate the advent of golden syrup. It is likely that molasses was used, very similar to medieval honey-breadcrumb gingerbreads, and I wouldn't be surprised if they were an offshoot of those ancient sweetmeats.

I have made many treacle tarts in my time, and I have found they are best made with some other flavours to cut through the intense sweetness. The classic is lemon juice and zest, but a couple of tablespoons of black treacle also works well, and I like to add a good spoonful of mixed spice. I read in a 1979 copy of the *Fanny Farmer Cook Book* that dark corn syrup should be used for treacle tart. I have to say a very loud 'No!' here. Golden syrup is the only choice. Accept no substitutions!

CHEESECAKE

Cheesecakes are not cakes but tarts, a mixture of some kind of soft cheese (curds or cream cheese usually), eggs, sugar, cream (fresh or soured) and sometimes a stabilising starch like cornflour or fresh breadcrumbs. The shell was originally always a pastry one, it's only when we reach the twentieth century that cheesecakes are made with a base of broken biscuits. The concept of a cheesecake is ancient, with references to them appearing in Roman texts. The earliest British example is the rather delicious-sounding 'sambocarde', an open coffyn-style tart, filled with a mixture of curd cheese, sugar, egg whites and elderflowers ('blomes of elrin') and rose water. Curds were the main form of cheese for cheesecakes right up until the nineteenth century, though they are little used today. One of the reasons for this is that it's difficult to buy curds that are the correct texture; many modern recipes say to use cottage cheese, but it is too rubbery. It is very easy to make, however. Here's an eighteenth-century method: 'Set a Quart of new Milk near the Fire, with a Spoonful of Runnet, let the Milk be Blood warm, when it is broke, drain the Curd through a coarse Cloth, now and then break the Curd gently with your fingers.'[20] 'Runnet' – or rennet – comes from the stomach lining of male calves, but these days a vegetable-based rennet can be used.

By the Stuart era, cheesecakes were more refined, baked in polygonal cases made by rolling a circle of dough, cutting nicks into the circumference at equal intervals, raising them and then pinching the edges together. Cheese, sugar and eggs were flavoured with such things as pistachios, dried fruit, sack (a sweet alcoholic drink, similar to sherry) and spices. The filling was poured in, an intricately carved pastry decoration tentatively placed on top and the whole thing was baked. The only place in the country still making and eating the traditional curd cheesecake in any significant number is Yorkshire, and the best place to purchase them is in the city of York. They are delicious, a mixture of curds, sugar, eggs, currants and a very good pinch of ground allspice.

In the eighteenth century, cheesecakes were being made without any cheese at all (though still plenty of other dairy products). Most famous of this kind are maids of honour. The recipe is a trade secret, but they are a cheese-less almond cheesecake typical of the time: a puff pastry case filled with a mixture of milk, breadcrumbs, butter, sugar, lemon zest, ground almonds and eggs. There's a lot of nonsense about them being invented for Henry VIII, but the recipe was developed by the royal court of a much later (probably Georgian) monarch and the palaces at Kew. The recipe was purchased by the Newens in the nineteenth century, who opened 'The Original Maids of Honour Shop', which is still open today and sits opposite Kew Gardens. They are rarely made by anyone else these days. Recipes do crop up in twentieth-century cookery books, but the pastry is shortcrust and the filling a dot of jam and some sponge cake batter. A shadow of its former self.

The best cheesecakes of the baked kind today come from the USA; the cheese of choice being a super-smooth cream cheese. It is easy to devise one's own fillings, as long as you keep to the basic rule of adding one egg for every 250 millilitres of filling. New York-style cheesecakes are easy to prepare, but actually quite difficult to bake, the most common problem being that the filling rises in the oven, soufflé-like, only to collapse once removed. Harold McGee has done some troubleshooting for us to avoid this problem: first of all beat the ingredients carefully, so as not to incorporate any air bubbles; bake it slowly, in a water bath in a low oven, and leave it to cool gradually by turning off the oven and opening the door; but most importantly of all – don't overbake it! A cheesecake filling is essentially a custard, so it is ready when the centre is still quite jiggly.

The best cheesecake I have ever baked is one from a recipe given by John Farley, a delicious combination of cream cheese, cream, orange flower water, egg yolks, melted butter, ground almonds, sugar and crushed macarons. I highly recommend searching out the recipe in his book *The London Art of Cookery*, published 1783.

ECCLES AND BANBURY CAKES

Eccles cakes are round 'cakes' of flaky pastry filled with a mixture of dried fruit, spices, sugar and melted butter. They have their own creation myth (*of course* they do), and this one surrounds the great eighteenth-century cook and entrepreneur Elizabeth Raffald. The story goes that she made an early iteration of them in her Manchester shop in the latter half of the eighteenth century. When a member of her kitchen staff left her employment, she took the recipe with her and made a killing selling them in Eccles. These proto-Eccles cakes were called 'Sweet Patties', made of flaky pastry stuffed with dried fruit, etc., but also chopped apples, a bit of booze and the meat picked from boiled calf's feet left over from the jelly-making process. If anything it is a mince pie, and to say that it was the forerunner to the Eccles cake requires, as Laura Mason and Catherine Brown put it, 'a stretch of the imagination'.[21] The first recipe for a bakery product called an Eccles cake doesn't appear until the nineteenth century, but they were certainly being made in Eccles in the 1790s by James Birch, who owned a bakery on Eccles high street. They were probably sold as a traybake: two layers of pastry filling with the fruit mixture, rather like currant slices, or 'dead fly cemeteries' as they were often called by children. Birch's shop was a great success and he quickly moved to larger premises across the road. An ex-employee of his, William Bradburn, immediately filled the vacant space and started selling them too. The cheek of it. At one point Bradburn was selling 8,000 cakes per day and Birch sold 5,000 per day. Birch must have been fuming.

There is also the somewhat plainer, but larger, Chorley cake, made from shortcrust pastry and filled with less fruit. They are 'regarded by some as a poor relation of Eccles cakes'[22] but there are other, similar cakes made around the country that are less well-known, including Shrewsbury simnels and Coventry godcakes.

The cake of this sort with the longest legacy is Banbury cake, which is even richer than the Eccles cake. They are oval in shape, with a crunchy crust of granulated sugar. The first bakery to sell them opened in 1638, and the earliest recipe for them dates to the 1610s. The recipe appears in *The Compleate Cooke* by W. M. (first published in 1658) and is titled 'The Countess of Rutlands Receipt of making the rare Banbury Cake which was so praised by her Daughters'.[23] It is made from a yeasted dough, half of which is enriched and mixed with dried fruit, ambergris, musk and rosewater – the aromas emanating from the oven must have been quite the heavy hit! The enriched dough was then sandwiched between two layers of plain dough.

It seems to me that the predecessor of all of these dried fruit and pastry cakes were simple turnovers and traybakes, and were rather modest. A good example of this is the Yorkshire mint pasty, a mixture of dried fruit, sugar and a little chopped mint baked in a plain lard and butter shortcrust. The addition of a little fresh mint to fruit is a delicious and forgotten Yorkshire flourish. I recommend bringing it back, especially in fresh fruit pies.

FILO PASTRY

Of all the types of pastry to attempt to make at home, filo seems to be the most nightmarish. It is like puff pastry in that, once baked, there are several layers of thin, crisp pastry.

With filo, though, the layers are not achieved with rolling and folding ever-increasing layers of butter and paste, but it is instead made into large, single layers that are then stacked. It has many uses, but the two best known are for baklava and strudel. It evolved in the Turkish Ottoman Empire from a layered bread made in eight thin layers of dough, but it wouldn't be until the sixteenth century that the technique for paper-thin dough was developed.

The dough is made of flour and water in an approximate three-to-two ratio, with a little oil and salt. The dough is kneaded very well by slapping, stretching and folding it repeatedly for around fifteen minutes – sounds very satisfying and possibly therapeutic. Before the big stretch begins it is rested overnight. The next day, it is rolled out thinly, then placed on floured cotton sheets where it is pulled and pummelled with blunt knuckles – fingers are too pointy – and when it begins to get really thin, it is stretched further by spreading the hands beneath the cotton sheets. This is a two-person job at least, and the grand houses of Istanbul always employed two filo chefs. The pastry is so thin that newspaper can be read through it – a thickness of 0.1 millimetres. It is a sight to behold watching skilled pastry cooks make such a devilishly difficult pastry, a feat of skill, coordination and communication. The pastry is prone to breaking once made, so if you do use it at home, cover your stack of thin pastry sheets with a damp tea towel, and as you use it, brush each sheet with melted butter, or it will crumble to shards.

Baklava predates the invention of filo pastry by centuries, and it was first made from sheets of a pasta-like dough, not unlike lasagne sheets, but the switch to filo was made as soon as it was invented, it seems. Baklava is made by sandwiching several layers of filo with a sweet filling, usually ground or chopped nuts including almonds, pistachios, walnuts and even peanuts. Less known are the fruit curd fillings, which offer a contrasting tart flavour to the sweet honey or sugar syrup in which the baklava is soaked after baking.

The Ottoman Empire came to stretch all the way to Austro-Hungary and, of course, filo pastry went with it. The empire receded, but the pastry remained, in the form of strudel. They are made by spooning cold, stewed fruit – usually apple – onto the edge of a square of several stacked filo sheets and swiftly rolling it into a sausage, ends tucked under. The word strudel means 'eddy' or 'whirlpool' in German for this reason. It is placed on a baking sheet in a horseshoe shape (otherwise it wouldn't fit in the oven), brushed with melted butter and sprinkled with breadcrumbs and baked. So proud is Austria of its dessert that, along with its similarly famous Sachertorte, it is used extensively on tourist guides and advertisements to tempt holidaymakers to the country. Wherever it went, the empire took its thin pastry, and it was also taken up and adapted in other countries, such as India for samosas and China where it is used for spring rolls, which you could argue are an example of a tiny, savoury strudel. The old, rather obscure Ottoman Empire actually had a significant influence upon the food we all eat today.

AMERICAN PIES

One of the best days of my life was the time I walked into the House of Pies bakery in Houston, Texas, back in 2010. It was a sight to behold; scores of shelves filled, perhaps even groaning, with wonderful, large and generously filled pies. I lived in the USA for two years and spent the majority of my time in the Southern States, so I will focus on the best-known pies from that part of this vast country.

The USA is known for its fruit pies – apple, cherry and blueberry – but the pie of the South is most certainly peach, it being the perfect climate to grow the fruit. North Americans make their fruit pies differently to the British in that raw fruit (and sugar and spices, etc.) is put directly into the pie shell. This can make the filling watery, and the pastry bottom rather soggy. To combat this, a scattering of cornflour goes on the pastry base before the fruit is added, and more is sprinkled over the fruit filling. The pie is covered and put into a very hot oven to crisp the base quickly. Inside their pies, the cornflour mixes with the juices, making a sauce. The result is a pie much fresher in taste than the British pies made with pre-cooked fruit.

Pecan pie is the official pie of the state of Texas, it being excellent pecan country. However, the first commercial pecan trees were not native to the state. They were grafted in the 1840s by an enslaved gardener called Antoine at the Oak Alley Plantation in Louisiana. Decades after his death, the nuts from his grafted trees won 'Best Pecan' at the

Philadelphia Centennial Exposition. Pecan pie is an integral part of the traditional American Thanksgiving meal, but it only found itself there since the 1930s, the result of a very successful advertising campaign by *Karo* brand corn syrup. Not very romantic, but there you go.

My favourite North American pie by far is Florida's state pie, key lime pie. The filling sits somewhere in between set custard and fruit curd. It is traditionally made with eggs, tinned sweetened condensed milk and the juice and zest of tiny key limes, the condensed milk being a hangover from a time when there was no refrigeration. It is unlikely that you'd have real key limes in your pie these days, even if you were in Florida, because they are very difficult to grow commercially. Instead, regular limes are supplemented.

The official pie of Mississippi state is, unsurprisingly, Mississippi mud pie, and it is possibly the dessert that hits the richest, hardest punch of all chocolate cakes. Looking into its history is somewhat confusing, and there are mentions of it being named after the mud left behind in the great flooding of the state in 1927. The trouble is, the earliest mentions are as recent as the 1980s, and when you do see descriptions and recipes, no one can decide on what this pie *is*: one recipe was essentially pecan pie with some cocoa powder mixed into it, and others are simply moist chocolate sponges with an extra-gloopy ganache covering. My theory is that many desserts have been given the name, and seeing as the USA has so many rich, unctuous and messy-to-eat chocolate confections, the name would have been an obvious one to choose. But one form did win out, and it's the ultimate chocolate hit: a chocolate pastry or biscuit base with a thick layer of a chocolate-brownie-like mixture, a rich chocolate mousse poured over it, topped with whipped cream and decorated with – of course – chocolate curls. Death by chocolate has nothing on this pie.

WHAT IS A PUDDING?

The most read post on my long-running blog by quite a margin is entitled 'What is a pudding?' Pudding is a difficult word to pin down because it means different things to different people. It's especially difficult for those visiting England, and this repeated question from non-Brits was the prompt for writing the post in the first place. Pudding can be a byword for dessert. Some are baked (though they are in the minority), others are steamed or boiled, or cooked on the hob. Then there are the savoury ones: steak and kidney pudding, Yorkshire pudding and black pudding – how come they're all puddings as well? To answer this question, we need to take a historical step back to find the origin of this seemingly catch-all term.

The original puddings were mixtures of various kinds, stuffed into animal intestines and then poached. Sometimes they were fried after poaching. Typical ingredients were meat or offal, fat such as backfat or suet, something starchy like barley, oats or breadcrumbs, as well as various herbs and spices. Sometimes these mixtures were cooked in a stomach, like a haggis, Robert Burns' 'chieftain o' the pudding-race'.

Puddings such as these have been made since ancient Roman times at least, but the word 'pudding' appears to come from the French *boudin*, i.e. a poached sausage like *boudin noir* or *boudin blanc*. It may surprise you to know that rice pudding and bread-and-butter pudding have their origins in animal guts.

Making puddings in intestines is great from the point of view of nose-to-tail eating, but it does mean that you have to wait for an animal to be slaughtered *and* have access to those animals. In the Middle Ages, this kept pudding a high-status food. However, in the mid-seventeenth century, there came an innovation in pudding technology, the pudding cloth. It might not sound that ground-breaking, but it was: it didn't require animals to be slaughtered and it could be reused. Fillings were tied up and boiled in it, forming those cannonball-shaped puddings like those depicted in Charles Dickens stories. In Scotland the clootie dumpling was made, a close cousin to the Christmas pud, cooked at Hogmanay in a pillowcase. Now everyone could enjoy pudding, though the fillings were perhaps less ostentatious, making good use of cheap flour, left-over breadcrumbs, suet and currants or treacle for sweetness, if they could be afforded. Then, at the end of the seventeenth century, came pudding moulds. At first they were expensive and intricately shaped (people often mistakenly think they are jelly moulds today), but simpler and cheaper pudding basins were ubiquitous before long. Other foods, such as jelly, blancmange and ice cream, then began to be included as puddings, because they too were made in moulds.

It is only in the eighteenth century, with the invention of the range oven, that we see a significant number of puddings adapted for the oven: steamed sponge puddings become baked sponge puddings, and the Yorkshire pudding shifted from cooking underneath the roasting meat as it turned on its spit, to a tray in a hot oven. Many puddings have only ever existed as baked products: Eve's pudding and sticky toffee pudding being two examples. Manchester and Bakewell puddings are cooked in a pastry shell, and are technically pies or tarts really, unless we are counting the pastry shell as the vessel inside which the pudding is cooked.

By the Victorian era, the upper classes were eating lots of expensive desserts: ice creams, jellies and exotic fruits, but they still wanted simple puddings over everything else. In fact, on weekdays when there were no visitors, a couple of puddings was often the only choice at lunch or dinner. This is why the dessert course became known as the pudding course. As the price of spices and sugar dropped through the nineteenth and into the twentieth century, plain suet puddings could become richer and richer, the pinnacle for many folk being sticky toffee pudding – possibly the most indulgent of all of the puddings.

BAKEWELL PUDDING

'A great deal has been written on the history of the celebrated Bakewell Pudding, much of it I am afraid rather inaccurate nonsense.' Ivan Day[24]

Before we delve into the lore of this classic British sweet, I need to make sure we are on the same page here, because a Bakewell pudding is not the same thing as a Bakewell tart. The former is made of a puff pastry case in an oval or round tin, spread with jam, and filled around halfway with a mixture of egg, sugar, melted butter and ground almonds. It is very rich and most unlike the tart, made up of shortcrust pastry, almond-flavoured sponge and raspberry jam.

Precisely how this pudding became associated with the small Derbyshire town is unclear, and three independent establishments all claim to be the purveyors of the original pudding. The one story that seems to be most popular (this doesn't mean it is true, of course) is that it was made by accident, a mix-up in the kitchens of the Castle Inn, now called the Rutland Arms. The precise recipe is a secret, but twentieth-century food journalist Sheila Hutchins got hold of a recipe in the 1960s, apparently from the kitchen cook at the Rutland. The filling is straightforward and entirely predictable; a mix of eight ounces each of sugar and melted butter, eight eggs and four ounces of ground almonds.

There has been much confusion about the pudding's heritage, but food historian Ivan Day has done a great deal of detective work in this area.[25] The earliest recipe was thought to be in Eliza Acton's *Modern Cookery for Private Families* in 1845. After much searching, Ivan discovered an earlier recipe in an 1837 edition of *Family Magazine*, printed not in England, but in Boston, USA. He later found that the recipe had been copied from a British magazine, printed the year before. Then, a recipe, handwritten by a Mrs Norton, and dating to 1835 turned up. It turned out she was a cook with links to the Castle Inn, Bakewell! In these very early days the Bakewell pudding was still finding its feet. Food historian Glyn Hughes also found a recipe for the pudding dating to 1837; it had no pastry and was a mixture of egg, butter and sugar. Before the mixture was poured into its buttered tin, the bottom was strewn with dried fruit and candied peel and cherries. This description is almost identical to another pudding, dating to the previous century, called sweetmeat cake, and it is most likely to be the true origin of the Bakewell pudding. Sweetmeat cakes were part of a tribe of puddings called transparent puddings, so called because when cooked the rich filling, a mixture of egg, sugar and butter, sets clear, and they are most delicious. Later in the century, they were baked in fashionable puff pastry, then, to become a Bakewell pud, all that had to happen was a swap of candied fruit to cheaper raspberry jam, creating a pudding with more commercial potential. It doesn't explain how the association with Bakewell came to be, and food writer and historian Regula Ysewijn is probably correct in writing that it 'was an existing pudding that was renamed thus to attract customers in the nineteenth century'.[26]

'A genuine Bakewell Pudding,' wrote Sheila Hutchins, 'bears little relation to the dish made in the South of England … Bakewell Tart.'[27] Many folk believe it to be a dumbed-down version and recipes start to appear at the turn of the twentieth century. By the 1920s, the Bakewell tart has ousted the pudding (for those outside of Derbyshire, that is), and a 1923 edition of *Mrs Beeton's Cookery Book* gives a recipe for Bakewell tart with an almond sponge. If you look up 'Bakewell Pudding' in the same volume, the entry simply says 'see Bakewell tart'. Oh dear. This cheap version was quickly pounced upon by food factories, including Mr Kipling, who created the cherry Bakewell with its hideous, oversweet sponge, thick layer of white icing and glacé cherry. The tart can be a wonderful thing if the over-sweet dry sponge is replaced with frangipane, proper almond extract is used, and the base is spread with a good, tart raspberry jam, and *absolutely no icing*!

CRUMBLES, COBBLERS AND SLUMPS

Everyone loves a crumble. Its close cousins the cobbler and slump are pretty good too. You could say that these fruity baked puddings are pie-adjacent, because any filling used in a crumble can also be baked as a pie. Crumbles are better than pies in my book, and they are much easier to make too. Wrote Jane Grigson in her *Fruit Book* (1982) of her apricot and almond crumble: 'It is always a great success with our French and Italian friends, who ask for an English pudding but whose pioneering spirit would fail if faced with Spotted Dick or Dead Man's Leg [roly-poly pudding].'[28] To make a crumble, fruit is stewed with sugar, sometimes flavoured with spice, favourites being apple (perhaps with added blackberries), gooseberry and rhubarb. Cooked and cooled, this filling is poured into a baking dish and covered with the topping, essentially a sweet pastry mixture without any liquid (water or egg) to hold it together. To make the topping, butter is rubbed into flour before sugar is mixed in (I find granulated or Demerara the best). A good rule of thumb is two-parts flour to one-part butter, and one-part sugar, though the precise amount of the latter can be adjusted to the tartness of your fruit. As it cooks in the oven, clumps of topping begin to bind, but only just, the texture of which, says Laura Mason, 'can only be described as crumbly'.[29]

Crumbles are easy to make, but they can go awry when the top ends up becoming a rather soggy mess. This occurs for two reasons: the first is that there isn't enough crumble topping; you always get a slightly gloopy layer at the crumble-fruit interface, so you need to account for that. The other reason is that the fruit layer is too wet – this is especially an issue if the fruit is being baked from raw. It is always best to cook the fruit ahead of time, and if it is on the liquid side, you can drain away the excess (don't throw it away – drizzle it on top of the crumble if you're serving it with cream). It's also a good idea to be inefficient with your rubbing in – you need some rubble in that crumble mixture, not just fine sand. I find that adding some rolled oats to the mixture helps here, and I even bake the crumble ahead of time to keep that gloopy layer to a minimum.

Researching for this part of the book, I found no crumble recipes in any cookery books or magazines prior to the 1970s, and it seems that what I thought to be the most British of puds actually came to us from the USA during the Second World War. New recipes take a while before they are found reproduced in cookery books – on average, 25 years, it is said – so that we don't find recipes in British cookbooks until the 1970s fits quite well. There are other desserts similar to the crumble, such as brown Betty, with its crumble made of breadcrumbs, dark brown sugar and melted butter, which seems to have appeared in the Southwest United States in the opening decade of the twentieth century.

Older than the crumble is the cobbler, its topping made from a sweet scone mixture. The earliest mention of one I could find is in the *Report of the Missouri State Horticultural Society for the Year 1808*, where a discussion on seasonality and the produce one can look forward to talks of peach trees 'and anticipations of the melting peach cobbler in the near future'.[30] In a New England version of the pudding, the 'cobbles' are broken and pressed into the fruit in an action called 'dowdying'.

Oldest of all – yet newest to the UK – is the slump, apparently conceived by Louisa May Alcott, author of *Little Women* (1868), who placed pieces of leavened sweet dough over fruit, the dough rising and then slumping as it bakes. I find it heart-warming that desserts that have come from other countries have been accepted into the broad church that is the British pudding.

BAKED CUSTARDS

Delicate just-set baked custards are one of my most beloved baked puddings because they include both *crème brûlée* and *crème caramel*. You could be forgiven for assuming that a baked custard is just a custard tart without its pastry shell, but this sort of pudding arose via a different path – from boiled puddings. Custards sometimes stabilised by some flour were tied up in a pudding cloth, boiled, and gingerly turned out onto a dish. There's a recipe for 'a Cream Pudding to be Boiled' in Robert May's *The Accomplisht Cook* (1685) that is made from eggs, cream, sugar, almonds and rose water. These sorts of puddings became known as quaking puddings. At the very end of the seventeenth century, we find the recipe for crème brûlée in a French cookery book by F. Massialot called *Le Cuisinier roial et bourgeois* (1692). Only in the eighteenth century do we see recipes for it in British cookery books, except that it goes by the name 'burnt cream'. At this time the custards were set in a way we might consider cheating today, because the custard contains a lot of flour and is thickened in a pan, over a hob – essentially a *crème pâtissier* – and poured into a dish and scattered with an even layer of sugar. Elizabeth Raffald, writing in 1769, tells us 'to hold a hot Salamander over it 'till it is very Brown, and looks like a Glass Plate put over your Cream'.[31] A salamander is a very hot grill, with a red-hot belly like that of the Eurasian newt. Today, we would use a chef's torch, though you do get a better, more even glass-like top if you use a proper, old-fashioned grill.

By the second half of the eighteenth century, some custards were being set in hot water either in ovens or close to the fire, and Elizabeth Raffald, always with her finger on the pulse of cooking and food fashions, provided a recipe for 'Orange Custards', a custard made without stabilising flours and flavoured with Seville orange juice and zest. She tells us to 'set them in an Earthen Dish of hot Water, let them stand 'till they are set, then take them out … serve them hot or cold'.[32] They are delicious and the first historical recipe I ever made.

Crème brûlée also goes under the name of 'Trinity cream', and it is often served for pudding at Trinity College, Cambridge, with the college's crest branded into the sugar top. The story goes that an undergraduate from Aberdeenshire offered up the recipe, but it was turned down because the chap, being just an undergraduate, was considered to be too lowly to be making such suggestions. Several years later, he would become a Fellow and the decision was reversed, the name of the Scotsman conveniently not given.

The cousin of the crème brûlée is surely the *crème caramel*: a set custard with a caramel layer cooked beneath it. Before it goes in the oven, a vanilla custard is poured into a mould or moulds already containing a set-hard layer of caramel, which softens and merges deliciously with the setting custard.

The innovation that allowed custards to be made so much more delicately was the water bath – or, if you prefer, *bain-marie* – which cooks food much more gently than the direct heat of the stove or oven. Custards sit in their ramekins which are, in turn, sitting in very hot water (straight-sided roasting tins are good for this task) and baked, uncovered, at a low temperature. The water they are sitting in never gets hotter than 100 degrees Celsius (if hotter, then it is steam, and not liquid water anymore). At the same time, the hot water is cooled by the process of evaporation from its surface, dampening the temperature inside the bath for a more gentle and even bake (we experience this effect when water on our skin evaporates, making us chilly).

One type of set custard that was thought to be very nourishing for the ill was called 'Seftons', named after the first Earl of Sefton. These are savoury custards made from eggs and stock and set in the oven, often served with toast. For some reason they have been forgotten – a great shame because if made properly with good stock flavoured with a little lemon juice, they are delicious. Honest.

YORKSHIRE PUDDING

The simple combination of Yorkshire pudding and roast beef makes up the National Dish.* A savoury, baked batter pudding whose honours and traditions are proudly kept by the people of Yorkshire. However, if you delve into the history of this pudding, these ideas quickly evaporate. The earliest printed recipe for Yorkshire pudding pops up in Hannah Glasse's 1747 classic *The Art of Cookery Made Plain and Easy*. The batter is the same as we use today, the difference is this pudding isn't baked, at least not in the sense we mean today. Glasse tells us to: 'take a Stew-pan and put some Dripping in it, set it on the Fire, when it boils, pour in your Pudding [batter], let it bake on the Fire till you think it is high enough,

---

* Several dishes vie for this top spot today: fish and chips comes in a close second followed by chicken tikka masala. For more information see 'The National Dishes of England, Ireland, Scotland, and Wales' by Elaine Lemm on *The Spruce Eats* website: www.thespruceeats.com/national-dishes-of-brita n-and-ireland-435493#:~

then turn a Plate upside-down in the Dripping-pan [place under the roasting meat] and let the Dripping drop on the Pudding, and … make it of a good fine brown.'[33] She doesn't specify the type of meat it should be cooked with, but it's not that far off the pudding we know and love. The trouble is, the recipe can be traced further back than this to a time when this pudding did not have an association with Yorkshire at all, when it was simply called a dripping pudding. Not only that, it was cooked beneath not a joint of beef, but a shoulder of mutton!

So how did a generic dripping pudding become associated with Yorkshire? Well, no one knows for sure, but my own research has led me to believe it is because of the *way* the people of Yorkshire ate it. You see, it became popular to begin the meal with Yorkshire pudding – with gravy, or sometimes with jam – the idea being that diners would already be full of pudding and would therefore eat less of the more expensive meat when it came to the main course.

Today we bake our Yorkshires in an oven and don't place them beneath a roasting joint, but they are still very delicious. There are many arguments to be had regarding the baking of the perfect pudding. I go with Yorkshire food writer Elaine Lemm's fool-proof recipe: equal volumes of plain flour, eggs and milk, plus a big pinch of salt. Allow everything to rest for a few hours, then get the fat (beef dripping, please) really hot in your tins, and pour in your batter deftly, shut the oven door and don't even think about opening it again for at least 25 minutes.

There is one thing I believe you must do to make the best Yorkshire pudding at home, and that is to avoid using muffin tins (if you want to be technical here batter cooked in these are popovers). No, you must take this advice from Yorkshire food historian Peter Brears: 'The true Yorkshire pudding is always made in a rectangular ... pan.'[34] I heartily concur; only then will you experience that combination of high, crisp edges and soft, pudding underbelly. The most economical of luxuries.

STICKY TOFFEE PUDDING

When it comes to baked puddings, the sticky toffee pudding must be the most loved. It is certainly one of the most popular. In my little restaurant, it never left my menu, and a cursory look on the internet shows that every celebrity chef you can think of has a recipe for it.

There are three contested origins of this pudding: one is that it was invented in 1907 by the landlady of the Gate Inn, Millington, Yorkshire. Another gives it a Scottish heritage, it being created in 1967 at the Udny Arms Hotel, Newburgh in Aberdeenshire. However, the most likely seems to be that it was the brainchild of chef Frances Coulson in 1948 at the Sharrow Bay Hotel, Ullswater, in the Lake District. He called it 'icky sticky toffee sponge'. The earliest reference I can find for the pudding in print is a *Guardian* article from 1976, which is about Mr Coulson and his hotel. In the article, Jane Grigson talks of Coulson's sticky toffee pudding, and of his approach to cooking in general in the 1940s and 50s: 'In those grey post-war days, the rich luxury of the cooking was a revelation of pleasure and gourmandise,' adding: 'if you had grown up, as I had, among people who thought it was a sin and a wicked waste to use butter and cream in cookery, his dishes shouted rebellion.'[35]

Recipes for the pudding these days are very rich, with piles of dark brown sugar, generous glugs of treacle and lashings of butter, but the original was less so, and all the better for it. The batter was very runny, with plenty of chopped dates, white sugar, self-raising flour, eggs and only a little butter. The very thin batter cooks to a very soft-textured sponge. Coulson's sauce was simply a case of boiling together cream and Demerara sugar until syrupy. My recipe is the same as Coulson's, except I make my sauce with the darkest brown sugar I can get and add a very large knob of salted butter to the molten mixture.

The pudding only really became popular in the 1990s, when there was a resurgence of traditional cooking, a time when real traditionalist cooks, such as *Two Fat Ladies'* Clarissa Dickson Wright and Jennifer Paterson, and Gary Rhodes, helped us look to our own culinary past and traditions for food inspiration. The sticky toffee pudding headed this resurgence, so much so that food critic A.A. Gill called it the 'black forest gateau of the 1990s'.[36] Helping the sticky toffee pudding on its way to stellar success is the Cartmel Village Bakery, also found in the Lake District, which has been pumping out thousands of puddings for nigh-on 30 years. The pudding has travelled too; in the 1990s a pastry chef from Illinois, USA, won a Bigalow Tea Award for 'best dessert for afternoon tea' with his sticky toffee pud.[37] It became popular again in the USA in the 2010s. In the same decade, it also became a trendy dessert in French restaurants. High praise indeed.

MANCHESTER PUDDING

There is a mind-boggling number of British puddings, many of them with minute differences between them. There is one tribe of baked puddings that are all made with a sweetened custard made stable by the addition of some breadcrumbs. The best-known of these puddings are Manchester pudding and queen of puddings. A Manchester pudding is a lemon-flavoured custard-breadcrumb *melange,* poured into a puff pastry case lined with jam and then baked. Queen of puddings is the same custard baked in a dish with no pastry, set, spread gingerly with jam, then topped with a simple French meringue and baked again. Are these puddings related – did one beget the other – or were they created independently? It's hard to tell, but Manchester pudding seems to be the oldest, but only just. The earliest recipe appears in *The English Cookery Book* published in 1859. The earliest recipe for queen of puddings appears in 1865 in Massey & Son's *Comprehensive Pudding Book.* Some people are of the opinion that queen of puddings was derived from Manchester pudding, and it is thought that the 'queen' in the name refers to Queen Victoria. Did a particularly delicious portion of the pud get served up to Her Majesty on a trip to Manchester? Did it receive praise from her and was then forever called 'queen of puddings'? The dates do check out to a royal visit to the northern city, but it seems unlikely. There are, for example, many other puddings that have received the moniker because they are simply delicious, and besides, as Regula Ysweijn points out in her book *Pride and Pudding* (2015), there are so many other puddings of that ilk, the chances of it being true are 'slim at best'. 'Be that as it may,' wrote historian Alan Davidson, 'queen's pudding [sic] in its modern form is one of the best British puddings.'[38]

Let's have a look at some of the other puddings of this tribe now we've met the two main players, and you will see just how difficult it is to try and piece together any sort of family tree: Chester pudding is the same as Manchester pudding, but 'with the whites of eggs frothed on top and lightly browned'.[39] Confusingly, Jane Grigson's Manchester pudding recipe has whisked eggs on top, simply because she considers it an improvement. Well, an improvement it may be, but it is no longer a Manchester pudding. Chichester pudding is the custard-bread mixture with whisked egg whites folded in only briefly, giving the finished dessert a two-tone, two-texture appearance, whereas Deptford pudding is the same but with the egg whites folded in thoroughly. Staffordshire Yeomanry pudding is the same as queen of puddings but with a richer custard. Then, there's a *second* Chester pudding, this time with an almond-flavoured custard baked in pastry (no jam) and topped with meringue. Food historian Glyn Hughes pointed out that there is a queen's pudding, which is different to queen of puddings because it's a set bread-custard served with a sweet fruit sauce, probably jam sauce. Last on my list is Monmouth pudding, a lemon-flavoured bread-custard, baked in a pastry case lined with apricot jam (not a different kind of jam, because that would be a Manchester pudding, of course). Interestingly, this pudding was also cooked by boiling in a cloth (without pastry or jam), so perhaps it is Monmouth pudding that is the true ancestor of these puddings.

THE DENBY DALE PIE

We end this chapter with the story of a unique food tradition, which I think sums up the British people and their respect for their heritage, no matter how bizarre and pointless it may be. The Denby Dale pie is a noteworthy pie tradition because of its ridiculousness. Made in the Yorkshire town, it was a huge communal pie, made only for the most special of occasions. The first time it was baked was 1788, a nice game pie, cooked by the landlord of the White Hart pub, to celebrate King George III recovering from his 'madness'. It was agreed that if another were to be made it would have to be bigger than the last, and so a tradition was created. The second was made in 1815, to mark Napoleon's defeat at the Battle of Waterloo. It contained two sheep and twenty fowls. The third, baked in 1886 to celebrate the repeal of the Corn Laws, was of an 'unprecedented' size, being made of 135 small furred and feathered game and poultry, five whole sheep, a calf and 45 kilograms of beef. Unfortunately, 'it came to a sudden end when its supporting platform collapsed and a crowd of 15,000 scrambled for pieces, demolishing it utterly and throwing it to the winds.[40]

The pie that was created for Queen Victoria's Golden Jubilee was even more of a disaster. It was a game pie that weighed in at an impressive 1.5 tons. When it was cut into – crowd watching expectantly – the foul stench of putrefying meat filled the air. It was caused, apparently, by the use of overhung game, which included, so they say, a dead fox. Never accepting the event itself to be a dud, the huge pie was carted ceremoniously through the town and given a proper burial under a good thick layer of pong-neutralising lime. Special commemorative funeral cards were sold to mark its passing.

The most recent Denby Dale pie was the Millennium Pie in 2000. It was such a behemoth that it had to be designed by the University of Huddersfield School of Engineering. The dish was 2.4-metres wide and 12-metres long and required five tons of beef, two tons of potatoes, one of onions and 200 pints of John Smith's bitter. One has to wonder what event would be so important to warrant another. I love this story, not just because it is amusing, but because it also shows just what people will do, the lengths to which they will go, to keep a tradition going no matter how difficult, eccentric or futile it is. Thank God for the folk of Denby Dale.

PATISSERIE

What is the difference between a traditional bakery in the British Isles and a French *pâtisserie*? Is there one? When we think of patisserie and desserts, we do tend to think of fancy, delicate, often elaborate work. Laura Mason defined the term patisserie as 'the French word for a pastry-cook's shop. In English this has come to mean, by extension, the goods in the shop, particularly fine and fancy small sweet cakes.'[1] Good pastry cooks are very much sought after and are paid handsomely for their skills, and it has been the case for at least the last 400 years or so.

Can we eke apart and separate the difference between British pastry and French *pâte*, pastry-cook and *pâtissier*, bakery and *pâtisserie*? Our tendency to elevate French cookery and cuisine above all others means that our perception of it is that they pay very close attention to detail, use difficult techniques and take greater pride in their rustic, country cooking. Bruno de Monte, Director of the highly regarded French culinary school Ferrandi Paris, wrote that 'pastry making is a profession that is both artistic and artisanal'.[2] British cooking, on the other hand, has been viewed as comparatively plain and simple, or at least superficially so – it doesn't mean it is boring, and it doesn't mean that it is easy; 'simple' refers to the fact that few ingredients are used, but are cooked well. In the eighteenth century, when there was a culinary war going on between French and English cookery styles, the 'plain and simple' cookery of old England was considered by writers such as Hannah Glasse and Elizabeth Raffald as something to be treasured, with Glasse referring to French chefs as wasteful 'boobies'. One also needs to take great attention to detail to carry it off well. The difference, perhaps, is that fewer and fewer of us are willing to pay for the skill and top-quality ingredients and are happier to purchase mass-produced preparatory foods over the well-made produce of the skilled baker.

There is a flipside to this French-improvement coin, however, because there are those who have been very snobbish about it, imposing French betterment and deriding British cooking as stodgy pap, fit only for podgy children, such as twentieth-century writers Elizabeth David and Fanny Cradock. To do this is a great mistake. In the 1970s Fanny Cradock urged us to make *petits fours* in her show *Fanny Cradock Cooks for Christmas*, even putting a whole episode aside to cover them. Her petits fours are just a variety of iced choux pastries, and they were reproduced by Cradock biographer Kevin Geddes: small eclairs covered with garishly coloured water icing. They look hideous, and I am sure that a *bona fide pâtissier* would have balked at them and would have much preferred a well-made shortbread or a slice of custard tart. Proper petits fours are beautiful: the term means literally 'little ovens', because they are essentially desserts as *hors d'oeuvres*: tiny tartlets, *mille-feuilles*, *financiers* and choux. This miniaturisation can just as easily be applied to British baking as to French, but then could we call it patisserie? I think we could, because the food has been elevated. Indeed, if you look in a book of patisserie, you will see recipes for shortbread or for pound cake; the difference is what is done to these foods and how they have been used artistically or how they have been combined with other preparations. There are several chefs and cooks over the years who have improved British cooking by applying some French methods. These include eighteenth-century cook and entrepreneur Elizabeth Raffald; chef to Queen Victoria Charles Elmé Francatelli; and twentieth and twenty-first century chef Gary Rhodes, and so, this is how I've approached choosing the topics inside these chapter: the more complex, elevated baked goods of French origin or inspiration.

CHOUX BUNS

Choux pastry is one of my great weaknesses, but I very rarely make it at home because more skill and judgement is required than your regular shortcrust. Consistent piping is essential, and the paste itself, which lies somewhere in between batter and dough, is tricky to make: a roux of butter, water and flour is made and cooked (but not for too long), and then just the right amount of egg has to be beaten in to achieve what the *Leiths Techniques Bible* describes as 'a reluctant dropping consistency',[3] whatever that means. It's one of those things you have to be shown how to make because so much judgement is required. Once piped, the dough is baked until puffed up and golden brown, then a few holes are made on their undersides, and they are returned to the oven so their insides can dry out. It's something that I have never got my head around: mine always puff up, but they always come out wonky and knobbly, and never a nice, round profiterole or slender éclair. I like to tell myself that mine might look like their original forms, because when the pastry was invented in the eighteenth century, the little buns came out round, but irregularly so, giving the pastry its name, *chou*, meaning cabbage.* The dough preceded the choux bun because it was only in the eighteenth century that someone had the bright idea to bake it; before then the paste was deep-fried to make beignets and little, round confections that went by the name 'nuns' farts'. Is choux worth making at home? Despite the negatives I have just listed, I would say yes; if only to appreciate the work and judgement required to make it, but also to experience a nice éclair, where the pastry is still crisp and not soggy like it is when purchased in a shop or bakery, where it may have been sitting for several hours, or even days.

The best-known choux product has to be the éclair, often filled with Chantilly or confectioner's cream of various types and flavours; in France chocolate and coffee are favourites. They might be topped with icing, ganache or *craquelin* for

---

* 'Mon petite chou' is a term of endearment in France, but it is not a reference to the vegetable, but the pastry; a better translation would be 'my little profiterole'.

crunchy contrast to the smooth cream. Then there are round profiteroles, filled with cream, or even ice cream and covered in warm chocolate sauce: a dessert very difficult to better. But for the *pâtissier*, these are just building blocks for more complex creations: *religieuses*, which means simply 'nuns', are made from two profiteroles, a large one makes the body and a smaller one sits atop for the head, secured with a flurry of ganache or streak of caramel, the whole thing decorated and adorned with various toppings. Often she is given a collar made from tempered chocolate. Then there is the very delicious *gâteau Saint-Honoré*; a circle of puff pastry, a circle of profiteroles glued around the edges with caramel, the centre filled with *crème chiboust*, a confectioner's custard with a meringue folded into it. It is unclear whether the gateau was named after Saint-Honoré, the patron saint of bakers, or the street the bakery was when it was conceived (Rue de Sainte-Honoré). I suspect both – surely a baker would want to open a shop on such a street. Most impressive of the choux creations is the *croquembouche*, made for special events, especially weddings; its name translates to 'a crunch in the mouth' because the high cone of filled profiteroles are glued together with caramel. The creation is smashed up by the bride and groom, making for quite the spectacle.

The best of the British choux creations is surely the simple choux bun: a very large profiterole filled with Chantilly cream and covered in chocolate or caramel icing. They immediately take me right back to the 1980s, and the 'Naughty, but Nice!' advertising campaign on television; it was an exercise in high camp, with celebrities such as Barbara Windsor, Larry

Grayson and Les Dawson devouring cream buns before speaking the saucy tagline 'Naughty, but nice!' The ads were funded by the Milk Marketing Board and National Dairy Council. The tagline was written by Salman Rushdie, of all people, and the whole campaign couldn't have undermined French sophistication and pride more.

GALETTES AND PITHIVIERS

In Britain the word 'cake' can mean many things: a Victoria sandwich for teatime, a toasted teacake in a café, Kendal mint cake on a hike. In French there is also a word used in many contexts and that is *galette*. Galettes were simple hearth cakes that have changes and diverged over time. In Brittany a galette is a buckwheat pancake, but more generally they are considered to be flat, round cakes; in fact the word galette is thought to come from the Old French *galet*, meaning 'flat pebble'. The type of galette you'll find in the patisserie is the seasonal *galette des rois*: cake of kings. It is made from two rounds of puff pastry and sandwiched between them is either a rich almond frangipane or *crème pâtissière des almonds*. Just as important is the dried fava bean, for this gateau is traditionally eaten on Twelfth Night and the finder of the bean would be king for the day – exactly the same thing used to happen in Britain with the iced Twelfth cake. More soberly, the king cake is representative of the three wise men who came to Jesus to give their famous trinity of gifts. One should be wary of any custom that is said to be pre-Christian, but in this case it does seem to be true, and this custom of a bean-king appears to go back to the ancient Roman feast of Saturnalia, a feast that had many customs reappropriated by Christianised Romans. One thing that doesn't go back very far is the 'traditional' delicious almond filling – an invention of the 1960s.

In New Orleans, a pithivier is made and eaten on Twelfth Night. It is almost identical to a galette des rois: two rounds of puff pastry and a frangipane filling, but enriched with a good dash of rum. It originated in the town of Pithiviers, just south of Paris. It is made in the shape of a flower, the central filling more pronounced and dome-shaped than a galette des rois. The edges are sealed and notched with a knife to make a flower-petal edging before being 'knocked up'. Knocking up is the action of making several shallow slashes in line with the cut edge of a pastry or pie, and it helps the edges rise well in the oven; trimming pastry, especially puff pastry, seals the edges, preventing it from rising well, and knocking up is a way of countering this. Pithiviers are known for their striking spiral pattern and deep, shiny egg glaze. The pattern is simple to do: it's a case of lightly marking the dome with the point of a knife from the centre to the edge in a slight curve, the marks can then be repeated as the thing is turned around. For the egg glaze, two egg yolks are beaten with half a teaspoon of salt, which sounds like a lot; you won't be able to taste it, but when the pithivier bakes, the proteins in the egg and the salt interact to turn especially dark and glossy. Only once you have glazed the top should you mark out your pattern with a knife, otherwise you'll paint over your beautiful pattern.

I have a third tip for making the best pithivier and you will think it very strange. It comes from Jane Grigson, who liked to add a minced, raw pig's kidney to her frangipane. 'Nobody will be able to guess what gives the delicious almond filling its interesting, nutty texture,' she wrote.[4] I have tested it out on diners in the past and I can confirm it to be true.

CONFECTIONER'S CUSTARD

Whether cooking British or French bakes, confectioner's custard, pastry cream, *crème pâtissière* – whatever you want to call it – will be required at some point. It is an egg-yolk custard stabilised with plain flour, and sometimes cornflour, to produce a stable, pipeable product. To make it, a custard is made with 500 millilitres of milk, six egg yolks, 125 grams of sugar and between 70 and 90 grams of flour, depending upon thickness required. The mixture is boiled – usually a big no-no in custard-making, but it is required to release and cook the starch contained in the flour. Finally, 150 millilitres of double cream is beaten in and the whole thing left to cool. This basic custard is useful for so many dishes: éclairs, custard slices (or if you must, *mille-feuilles*), or it is folded with egg whites and flavouring to make a sweet soufflé. The recipe, or least the proportions used, have never really changed since the first recipes in the very-late seventeenth century. Some are richer, like Francatelli's recipe that involved crumbling in ratafia biscuits, and adding orange flower water and brown butter. There is essentially one type in Britain, which some say is inferior to the French 'crème-pat' because the custard isn't quite as luscious, the British custard having more flour, fewer yolks and no cream. I'm not sure how fair that is; there are many French crème pâtissèrie recipes that ask for custard powder, so I think this is yet another example of food snobbery. The big difference is that in France, confectioner's custard is merely the starting point, it being used for a variety of other creamy elements. The main ones are *crème madame*, which is a crème-pat with whipped cream folded through it, and *crème diplomat* is the same, but with the addition of stabilising gelatine. *Crème chiboust* is a crème pat and whipped egg whites, invented by nineteenth-century master confectioner M. Chiboust for his gâteau Saint-Honoré, which was able to hold its shape for prolonged periods without gelatine; that said, more recently, when foods are made with longer shelf lives, *crème Saint-Honoré*, a chiboust with extra gelatine, was created. *Crème mousseline* has whipped butter mixed in; *crème crémieux* is the same but – again – with added gelatine. Lastly, *crème frangipane* is a crème-pat with an almond cream folded through it. This illustrates my point again that patisserie is the taking of basic elements and enhancing them by combining them with others or using extra processes. It makes the finished product more interesting and more expensive, of course, but it doesn't make one country's baking better than the others.

LET THEM EAT BRIOCHE!

One French bread that remains an indulgence is brioche, a loaf of white wheat flour enriched with egg and butter. The word comes from the French *broyer* meaning to 'break up', possibly in reference to the fact it breaks easily as a dough because of the high fat content. It probably originated in Normandy in the fifteenth century as an enriched bread, but true brioche as we think of it today was made in Paris from the seventeenth century, though it wasn't quite as rich as today's recipes; butter was particularly expensive at the time. Traditionally it is baked in one of two shapes: in deep, tapering fluted tins or as *brioche à tête*, which look like cottage loaves. The dough takes a long time to make; usually three provings are required in very cool, preferably refrigerated conditions, slowing, but not stopping, the fermentation of the yeast, while making the dough itself easier to handle.

Because of its high egg and butter content, the brioche sits somewhere in between cake and bread, and it has been confused for cake in the past: in the throes of the French Revolution, when Marie Antoinette apparently said of the peasant class 'Let them eat cake', what she allegedly said was *'Qu'ils mangent de la brioche'*. At the time, wrote Alan Davison, brioche was 'only lightly enriched ... and not very far removed from a good loaf of bread'[5] and would certainly not have been part of any dessert course. Not that it matters so long after the Revolution, but she might well have never actually uttered those words in the first place. The phrase and the story of a rich and entitled noble asking why the poor don't just eat some kind of fancy bread goes back to sixteenth-century Germany. So either the ill-fated queen didn't say it, or perhaps – as I like to imagine – she said it as a tongue-in-cheek, albeit misplaced, ironical joke.

BABAS AND SAVARINS

One of the very best products of the pâtisserie is the beautifully syrupy, rum-soaked, cream-filled *savarin*. If you are lucky the syrup will be flavoured with kirsch. These delicious enriched yeasted batter cakes are derived from the baba, an enriched dough containing dried or candied fruits baked in a tall, slender mould. Its origins are Slavic and medieval; a twelfth-century chronicler with the splendid name of Saxo Grammaticus described a festival bread in a tall, slender tin that was almost the height of a person – and it's the origin of the name because *baba* (or *babka*) means 'grandmother' or 'old woman'. Its popularity spread to what is now Poland and Western Russia, and it was here that it was made with dried and candied fruits. Sometimes it was flavoured with cheese. It went to Central Europe and became the *kugelhopf*, that great ring-shaped bread traditionally eaten for breakfast on Sundays. It even got picked up by the Italians to become panettone. All of these breads require a deftness of touch, and in Poland only women were allowed to make babkas, the men considered too ham-fisted and not maternal enough to care for such delicate doughs.

The baba picked up its rum flavoured syrup in France, coming to Paris via the Alsace or Lorraine region. Only in the 1840s did two Parisian brothers, surname Julien, decide to make their babas in ring-shapes and then, after baking, soak them in boozy syrup, filling the ring with crème pâtissière and Chantilly cream. The batter is like a liquid brioche dough, and is very eggy, requiring eight eggs, 100 grams of butter and 30 grams of honey for every 250 grams of strong flour. The dough is kept light by melting the butter and adding it after the first proving, rather like a genoise sponge. If you want to make one at home, buy yourself a non-stick ring: these cakes stick! And I am speaking from personal experience here: a traumatic pop-up restaurant where rum babas were the dessert, and a sleepless night of baking batch over batch in greased aluminium tins, where no amount of butter was enough to prevent sticking and tearing. I vowed never again.

The brothers Julian named their creation after the great gourmand and magistrate Jean-Anthelme Brillat-Savarin. Some go a little further and suggest that he was the one who came up with the idea in the first place. Several other foods have been named after him, including a tartlet, a flan and a baked egg dish, but this is the only dish with a claim to be invented by him. A flight of fancy? Perhaps, but he does namecheck the baba in his classic gastronomic memoire *The Physiology of Taste* (first published in French in 1825), a book in which he is a self-appointed Professor of Gastronomy. In an essay giving advice to anyone reading wanting to become plump, he recommended eating a variety of roasted meats, carbohydrates and eggs in the form of 'rice or macaroni, frosted pastries, sweet custards, creamy puddings, etc.' He also advocated sleeping a lot, and when it came to dessert he suggested going for 'Savoy biscuits, babas, and the other concoctions which are made of flour, eggs and sugar'.[6] I think I might have been following the advice of the professor all of my life.

CROISSANTS

The croissant is an icon, the pride of France, a beautiful sculpture worthy of Henry Moore, the apex of the pâtissier's skill. Croissants are made from a yeasted laminated dough, making them a sort of pastry-bread hybrid, a food that combines the best elements of both foods to produce something sublime. Properly made, they are a wonder of the modern world. They are traditionally eaten for breakfast with coffee, preferably in a Parisian café.

Such an iconic food needs an equally iconic origin story, so here goes. In the seventeenth century, Vienna was under siege from the Turks, who were making a good go at infiltrating the city by tunnelling their way in. They almost made it into a bakery, but the brave baker saved the day by making the tunnel collapse upon the invaders. His reward? He didn't want money – he was far too classy for that – he just wanted the right to bake special pastries, presumably of his own invention, to commemorate his involvement in ridding the city of the infiltrating enemy. These pastries were crescent-shaped, the symbol of the Islamic faith. We then have to assume he immediately ups sticks and travels to France to make them. The story is total hogwash, of course, but it was popularly perpetuated for decades, and it seems to have been concocted by writer Alfred Gottschalk, who 'recounted' the tale in the first edition of *Larousse Gastronomique* in 1938, a most trusted volume.

Food historian Laura Mason did trace the emergence of the croissant, and the earliest mention she could uncover dates to 1853, but there is no description of the food, and the first appearance of a recipe in print doesn't arrive until 1906. However, the pastry is not yeasted, and the first ones to be leavened don't appear until the 1920s – less than two decades before Gottschalk wrote the origin myth. Its rise to fame, then, is very much a twentieth-century story.

The French are a conservative nation when it comes to their foods and the way they are made and presented – absolutely nothing wrong with that, of course – and the croissant along with its variants – the almond croissant with its smear of marzipan and the *pain au chocolate* and its simple and understated finger of bitter chocolate – were the holy trinity never to be altered and never to be adorned. However, with the rise of *le fast food* from the 1970s, something that shocked and appalled many French folk, croissants were adapted, split and filled with ham and cheese to make melted sandwiches. The pâtissiers and café owners of France also obviously decided on the good old 'if you can't beat 'em, join 'em' strategy.

A really good croissant is increasingly difficult to find, and many – the majority – of them are factory-made with inferior products (I still eat them, of course). Proper croissants are not cheap, and to make them as they should be made requires time and lots of real, unsalted butter, preferably from Normandy. Croissant dough is made in the same way as a puff pastry, with strong flour so that the laminations can be built up with repeated rolling, folding and stretching – you don't want the dough layers to tear and merge. The paste itself is of similar hydration to bread, with an average hydration of 60 per cent, and like a bread dough, there is yeast. The process of folding and rolling is done between four and six times, each time the dough is rested in the refrigerator, then the croissants must be rolled, cut and shaped and proved at a low temperature that keeps the butter solid, but not so low that the yeast in the dough cannot produce its leaven.

The croissant's cousin, the Danish pastry, is made in a similar way, with a similar dough, the difference being that it's enriched with eggs and a little more butter is used. The dough is used in a greater variety of baked goods compared to that of the croissant. *Pain au raisin* is my favourite, and is probably the easiest to make, it being a rolled-up cylinder of dough spread with crème pâtissière, raisins and cinnamon, cut into slices, proved and baked.

The repeated folding and the slow proving of yeasted, laminated doughs means that it is only really viable to make them in large batches. It's a good idea to make at least double the quantity of pastries you want and freeze the remainder of them after they have been shaped and proved. Even then, when it comes to domestic production, I certainly sympathise with Elizabeth David, who wrote: 'I have to admit, though, that at the end of it all I do tend to suffer from combat fatigue, and question whether croissants are worth making at home.'[7] A domestic task for only the most committed of home bakers.

SUGAR

Sugar is probably the most used foodstuff in baking after flour, and it would be futile to try and describe all of the ways sugar is used in baking – I'd need a whole book for that. It is the pâtissier who uses sugar to its full potential; in the past, before the word pâtissier meant what it does today – i.e. pastry and dessert chef – the term used instead was confectioner. Today we would expect a confectioner to be making sweets, chocolates and candies, but going back a few centuries, when sugar was expensive, all sweet foods were considered part of the confectioner's culinary realm.

In the Middle Ages sugar was considered a spice and was used sparingly most of the time. However, for the members of the upper classes there were a few items of foods made entirely from sugar: sugar comfits and sugar plums (now called sugared almonds), which are still eaten today, especially at weddings. But it was in the subtlety course, a course of sculptures created from various foodstuffs, that the real cash was flashed, and the most prized of all were the sugar subtleties. Here sugar was mixed with starch or gum and poured into sheets of what was called sugar plate, or poured or pressed into moulds to produce some astounding pieces of art. For example, Catherine of Aragon (the first wife of Henry VIII) once had made a subtlety of a dungeon and manor house set atop marchpane (baked, hardened marzipan) complete with sugar swans and cygnets swimming in the moat. This theatre of the table wasn't eaten, it was far too expensive for that. However, by the time Elizabeth Tudor was on the throne, the price had dropped so much that she attended whole sugar banquets: hence her infamously black and rotten teeth.

It was quickly learnt that if sugar syrups were boiled to different temperatures and quickly cooled, the sugar would go through several different states and phases. Today it can be easily ascertained whether a sugar syrup has reached a certain state, as we can use a digital probe, but before thermometers different methods had to be used, and it was achieved by taking small drops of syrup and testing its consistency: soft, firm or hard; brittle or bendy. Each phase is reached at a specific temperature range, the first being 'thread', at a temperature of around 110 degrees Celsius. You can physically determine if this stage has been reached: 'Touch the surface of the boiling sugar with a dry finger. Join the thumb and this finger together and separate them. An elastic thread of sugar will be formed.'[8] Then there are the ball phases (112 to 130 degrees Celsius) when the syrup can be made into a ball with the fingers (before they have been dipped into iced water), and the very hot crack stages (132 to 154 degrees Celsius) come next, but at these temperatures, the syrup can no longer be made into a ball; instead it forms sheets that will crack when cold. Once a temperature of 160 degrees Celsius or more is reached, all of the water has evaporated away, and the sugar enters the caramel phase. Temperatures rise very quickly at this stage, and you mustn't take your eyes off the pan for a second because a caramel can go from a pale straw colour to bitter blackness in a matter of moments. In the process the sugar molecules are wrenched apart forming other aromatic and coloured molecules. At first caramels were made very pale, but as stove technology improved, allowing for better consistency and safety, caramels went the deep colours we would expect today. Below is a table of temperatures and states with examples of what they are used for in the patisserie.

Temperature	Term	Uses
106–13°C	Thread	Sorbets
112–16°C	Soft ball	Fondant icing and fudge
118–21°C	Firm ball	Soft caramel and toffee
121–30°C	Hard ball	Hard caramels
132–43°C	Soft crack	Butterscotch, nougat
149–54°C	Hard crack	Boiled sweets
160–77°C	Caramel	Brittles and praline

Adapted from *The Oxford Companion to Food*, Davidson, 1999.

It is easy to make these syrups if using a candy thermometer or digital probe; however, there are some things you need to bear in mind for success: use a heavy-based saucepan so the superheated syrup heats steadily and evenly; take the pan off the heat three or four degrees before the right temperature is reached – the pan will continue to heat the sugar off the heat; third, as the sugar boils it can rise up the sides and begin to crystallise, which could spell disaster and turn the whole lot back into crystalline form. Combat this by brushing around the inside of the pan with cold water throughout the boiling process. Finally, and most importantly, please be very careful!

WHISKS AND WHISKING, MIXERS AND MIXING

As a very amateur baker in the early 2000s, I was perfectly happy making cake batter with a wooden spoon, Chantilly cream with a balloon whisk, and meringues with my mum's old hand-cranked rotary whisk. But there came a moment when I had to upgrade to an electric stand mixer. They are essential for budding pâtissiers, because very often several different energy-demanding elements are required at the same time; what if you had to whip up a Swiss meringue, knead a sticky brioche dough and beat up some fluffy butter for a butter cream? Unless you have masochistic tendencies, you're not doing all of that by hand. What's remarkable is that most of these energy-consuming preparations predate the electric mixer, and some even predate the invention of the metal whisk. In the era of the Stuarts, you see recipes pop up for simple meringues of egg whites and sugar used to top pies; and there are recipes for 'snow' in Georgian cookery books (apples covered in a similar mixture) and there are dozens of cake recipes that require eggs and sugar to be beaten together often for up to an hour. Exhausting work – even more so when you discover these batters and early meringues were whisked with bundles of birch twigs (bark removed), reeds or bunches of birds' flight feathers. Wire whisks don't appear until the Victorian era; however, it is possible that they were around in the Italian Renaissance in the 1570s, because there is a lavishly illustrated book dating from this decade called *The Opera of Bartolomeo Scappi*, and if you look carefully at one illustration showing the various activities going on inside the dairy, there is one chap whisking the contents of a pot with something that looks exactly like a wire balloon whisk.

The first electric food mixer was invented by American Rufus M. Eastman in 1885, but it was essentially just a hand whisk cogged to an electric motor, and it didn't really catch on. Boom time came in the 1920s, when Frederick Osius and George Schmidt adapted one from a machine designed to beat milk and ice cream for milkshakes. It would prove very popular, but be quickly eclipsed by the iconic KitchenAid mixer. In its early development, the 'food preparer' was sent out to housewives, unnamed. Stuck as to what to call it, the testers were asked to suggest names for the device. When one tester said, 'I don't care what you called it, it's the best kitchen aid I've ever had', their problem was solved. They released their classic model in 1969 and the design hasn't changed since.

On the other side of the Pond, British inventor Ken Wood had established himself as creator of kitchen gadgets, finding some success making an electric toaster from abandoned radar and electronic equipment from the Second World War. He poured his profits into developing his Kenwood mixer. His genius was the addition of attachments that made onerous tasks, like can-opening and pasta-making, simple. For the home baker the revelation was the 'planetary action' of the mixer, which turned the whisks in one direction and the bowl in the other.

I must confess that I go for the KitchenAid, it is just a beautiful piece of engineering and design. I've been using mine for 25 years, and in the last 10 years it has seen heavy use, and I've never had to so much as oil it. It's not just endorsed by me, but also Julia Child and Nigella Lawson, who owns a very handsome steampunk-looking copper specimen. It's also the mixer used on *The Great British Bake Off*. One year they were swapped for Kenwood mixers, much to the shock of *Bake Off* fans. Kenwood has its high-profile fans too, with *Bake Off* judges Prue Leith and Mary Berry fighting proudly in its corner. Delia Smith loves her Kenwood too.

However, before you fork out for an expensive mixer, be aware that, despite mixers making life easier, the results are reckoned by some to be inferior to hand-whisking, producing a denser foam with less trapped air. I tried the balloon-whisk method once for Swiss meringue. Only then did I go out and buy the mixer; I don't mind slightly inferior meringues.

MERINGUES

The making of meringues is a key part of any baker's arsenal. Some are complex to make and are more likely to be made by a pâtissier, but they are all achievable for the home baker. A meringue is a light, aerated mixture of egg whites and sugar. There are other baked goods that are very similar, ones you could argue are meringues. I'm thinking of macarons and *jaconde* sponges, which have the addition of ground nuts. Indeed, it is from these sorts of cakes that true meringues were first created. The word meringue comes from the Italian word *meringa*, meaning 'evening bread', referring to little biscuits of whipped egg, sugar and nuts made into miniature loaves of bread, eaten as a novelty sweetmeat at the end of a meal. True meringues, using only egg whites and sugar, appear in the latter half of the seventeenth century, though they went by the name of 'sugar puffs'. The first recipe crops up in 1691, not bad considering at that point sugar came in sugarloaves and had to be ground finely in a pestle and mortar and the eggs whisked with twigs. Apparently, Marie Antionette loved making meringues, but then she also loved playing dairymaid – she had a special home dairy created just for her – so we might surmise that she liked *playing* at making meringues. Then as now they were shaped using spoons, but it wasn't until around 1800 that they were piped into myriad shapes and forms; the first person to do this was Antonin Carême, chef to the Prince Regent.

To make a good meringue you will need to use either caster or icing sugar, grains any larger won't dissolve into the egg white fully, resulting in a detectable grittiness. Undissolved sugar is also the cause of the weeping droplets that form in the final product. There are two broad categories of meringue: cooked and uncooked. The latter are the simplest, the most basic being egg whites whisked until they form stiff peaks (the meringue clings to the bowl if it is inverted), with sugar folded through with a metal spoon. French meringues are made by whisking egg whites with a little sugar until they form stiff peaks and then whisking in the remainder of the sugar spoon by spoon. A good rule of thumb is to use twice the weight of sugar to egg white. The longer the mixture is whisked and the slower the sugar is added, the glossier and firmer the meringue. If you must insist on making one with a balloon whisk, purchase a copper bowl to make it in. Copper ions leach into the egg white and provide stability to structural egg proteins, getting the job done much quicker and with considerably less elbow grease.

Cooked meringues have to be made with an electric mixer. A Swiss meringue is made by whisking eggs and sugar over a bowl of barely simmering water to a temperature of 75 to 78 degrees Celsius, and the partial cooking of the egg whites makes the final meringue much more stable. It is then taken off the heat and whisked until cold. Heating the eggs to this temperature effectively pasteurises them, making them safer to eat too. For an Italian meringue, egg whites are whisked and then a sugar syrup is heated to the soft ball stage (115 degrees Celsius), and it is trickled in a steady stream into the meringue as it is whisked with beaters on full power. Again, it is then beaten until cold. This meringue is very smooth and dense, and because of the extra structural integrity the boiled sugar has added to the meringue it can be happily stored in the fridge for up to five days.

Meringues can be baked very slowly at a temperature of 95 degrees Celsius, essentially drying out the mixture. Large meringues can be tricky to get right because the outside can dry out too much and discolour before the centre is done. This can be helped along by keeping the oven door open a tiny gap (use a wooden spoon) to expel the moisture. Meringues are a great insulator of foods – this is because of their air content – making them perfect for covering the ice cream in a baked Alaska. Cooked meringues can simply be waved over with a chef's torch.

Most commonly meringues are baked to make *vacherins*: these are commonly seen in the dessert aisle of the supermarket as simple meringue nests, which are easy to reproduce at home. A pâtissier, however, is able to pipe all sorts of complex, three-dimensional structures. However, my personal favourite example is rather homegrown: the Chivers 'Coronation Glory', the Imperial State Crown recreated in jelly and meringue. The recipe was created by the Chivers jelly company for housewives to make to celebrate the coronation of Queen Elizabeth II in 1953 (it's what she would have wanted, I am sure). It involved piping four long swirly lines of meringue on greaseproof paper sheets draped over a bottle or can and then baking them. Two jellies were then made: one large round one in a regular mould, and another in a tiny egg cup. The large one was turned out onto a plate and the smaller one fixed on the top with a rosette of pipe 'mock cream', looking dangerously nipple-like. More cream was piped around the edges, the four curved meringue pieces laid over the jellies just like the coronation crown, the whole decorated in silver balls and 'jewels' of candied angelica and glacé cherries. It's easy to mock such a creation today, but in 1953 the country was still coming out of food rationing, so to create such a thing at home must have been wondrous to those who were able. That's if anyone actually bothered to make one, of course.

PAVLOVA

Let's move to probably the most popular meringue dessert, the wonderful and versatile pavlova. It was famously named after the Russian ballerina Anna Pavlova in 1935, after her very successful tour of Australia. Of this we can be sure, but as usual, things get confusing. The naming of the dessert was done by chef Herbert Sasche, who was working at the Esplanade Hotel in Perth: the round and ruffled meringue supposedly represented a tutu. This is probably untrue, a post-hoc addition intended to add weight to an argument, because the people of New Zealand contest that the pavlova is actually a Kiwi invention. You see, while it was certainly named in Australia, the meringue was invented in New Zealand several years prior. This is very important, though, because one of the reasons the pavlova is such a good dessert is that special meringue with its marshmallow-like and slightly chewy texture, created by the addition of a small amount of cornflour and vinegar towards the end of the whisking process. It can be made with a straightforward French meringue, but you get the best results if you make a Swiss meringue: more gloss, and fewer weepy blobs of sugary syrup. Both countries are so sure of their personal provenance that they have both chosen the pavlova as their national dish.

Classic toppings for your pavlova are Chantilly or mascarpone cream plus fruit, either fresh or made into a curd with the yolks left over from the meringue-making process. The most popular include kiwi fruit, passion fruit, strawberry and raspberry, the latter most used in frozen supermarket pavlova, something for which I have a soft spot, I must admit.

The pavlova is involved in the creation myth of the popular British dessert Eton mess. The story goes that in the 1920s, during the school's annual cricket match, a rather giddy labrador sat on the picnic basket containing a large strawberry pavlova meant for the cricket tea, completely crushing it. The boys didn't care one jot that it was in such a state, and it was served up anyway, and the Eton mess was born.

You know the drill by now, reader: this is not true, it was actually invented by the school's cook in the 1930s, and if it was based on a pavlova, then the cook obviously realised that if serving it up quickly to hungry schoolboys it would end up a mess anyway – there's no neat way of doing it. But I think the pavlova is irrelevant to its creation. It's simply a huge fruit fool made of cream, fruit and jam with some broken meringues for texture. Maybe there were some meringue nests that needed using up, or some egg whites left over from custard-making. It's a creation not of a dog, but of an inventive member of Eton's kitchen staff.

MACARONS

One of the most elegantly simple items in the patisserie window are stylish *macarons*. At their most basic they are a baked mixture of whisked egg white and sugar and ground almonds, sitting somewhere between biscuit and meringue. It's only when you try to make them yourself do you appreciate the skill, effort and kitchen equipment required to pull them off well. And that's before considering the beautiful colours and flavour combinations of the macaron and the buttercream, jam or ganache filling. 'Ground almonds', wrote Arabella Boxer, 'were flavour of the month in the 1920s and macaroons were immensely popular, both for tea and for desserts, where they were used for the basis for soufflés and mousses.'[9] It was at this time that oven technology and precision cookware were available to produce them so consistently: almonds had to be ground to a fine powder, cooked meringues needed fast beaters, accurate thermometers and ovens with a consistent, even heat.

Macarons – or macaroons, as we only until recently spelt the word – first appeared in English cookery books in the late-seventeenth century, though they ultimately originate in Italy. They came to France in the 1530s after King Henri II married the wealthy Catherine de'Medici, who insisted upon them being cooked up at the French court. Anything new at court became instantly fashionable, and macarons spread throughout the land, and then to Britain. Basic recipes have changed very little; Elizabeth Raffald's 1769 book has instructions 'To make Makroons' that require equal amounts of egg white and sugar to be whisked, with ground almonds folded through the mixture. Almonds had to be pounded by pestle and mortar and were not as finely ground as we are used to today. They also required a sprinkling of rosewater to prevent them from turning into nut butter in the mortar. The technique was to pipe or spoon them in large, round, flat discs. They could be eaten at teatime, but they were commonly used in the base of trifles – no shop-bought Swiss roll or packet sponge fingers here! – or they were crushed to line soufflé dishes before baking. There is a diagram showing their shape in *Mrs Beeton's Book of Household Management* (1861). On the other side of the English Channel, technology was moving on: in the 1830s in France, almonds were being ground very finely, and Parisian chef Claude Gerbet began to make macarons in the small mounds we are familiar with today. He also worked out that allowing the piped macarons to dry for a short amount of time before baking produced the signature smooth top and risen edging.

If you ever fancy having a go at them yourself, it is a good idea to plan ahead, because according to Ferrandi Paris, really good macarons require whites that have been separated from their yolks four or five days beforehand – apparently it stops the whisked eggs from becoming grainy and prevents any water seeping from the whisked eggs. Italian meringue is the preferred base for macarons, making for a glossier final product, which is also less prone to cracking upon cooling than a French meringue. When piping, be prepared for the first few to be imperfect – it really is a skill one needs to practise. When they have rested and baked, they should be refrigerated for three days to firm up properly. This is why they are expensive; time is money, after all. Mrs Beeton's book contains a recipe for macaroons, and she wrote the following: 'We have given a recipe for making these cakes, but we think it almost or quite as economical to purchase such articles as these at a good confectioners.'[10] Some things have never changed.

FINANCIERS

The ebb and flow of fickle food trends are difficult to predict, and who would have thought the simple *financier* would suddenly receive its time in the spotlight? If you are not familiar with them, they are a type of sponge cake, made with a half-and-half mix of flour and ground almonds, whisked egg white and brown butter. They are baked in little rectangular pans, the shape of gold ingots, and look to me like a Brutalist interpretation of a madeleine. These finger-sized cakes are called financiers because they were designed, at some point in the 1880s, to be easily dipped into coffee, and there was no potentially messy creams and caramels that could drop on the smart clothes of the men of the Paris Stock Exchange. The almonds made them moist, and the butter made them indulgent. Sometimes they were flavoured with liqueurs like kirsch. The recipe was adapted from another cake that was a speciality of a house of nuns called the Sisters of the Visitation, who made large round cakes from egg whites, nuts and brown butter, called *visitandines*.

Financiers became very popular in France in the twentieth century because, along with other patisserie cakes like marble cake and madeleines, they travel well, being rather hardy and undecorated. These *gateaux des voyages*, as they were called, could be dispatched and delivered to cafés and restaurants where they may have been served as dessert with coffee, or with ice cream. It was a real money-spinner because financiers go stale rather quickly (and I am pretty sure they would be great in the base of a trifle) and they remained the pâtissier's speciality for decades. They have largely escaped mass-production in factory bakeries, unlike the poor madeleine.

CHOCOLATE

Whether it is to make ganache, a chocolate sauce or decorative curls for cakes, the pâtissier has to become *au fait* with the complex business of working with chocolate.

The first chocolate bars were not suitable for cooking with; in fact today we would probably think they were not fit for consumption because they were very grainy in texture. Joseph Fry was the first to produce them in 1847, and they were largely eaten as a health food. Chocolate was made by grinding cocoa nibs with cocoa butter, and other fats, into a paste and adding a bit of sugar. He used granite grinding stones but couldn't get the ground cocoa nibs (now cocoa solids) to a particle size of less than 0.03 millimetres; particles smaller than this cannot be detected by the human tongue. In Switzerland in 1880, confectioner Rodolphe Lindt developed a method for producing a smooth chocolate; he had invented the conche, a special grinder which took a shape reminiscent of the seashell. It worked by pushing the chocolatey slurry back and forth repeatedly between grinding stones, but it was only when the grinder was accidentally left on overnight that a super-smooth chocolate was made. In one happy accident modern chocolate was born.

If you are using chocolate in the kitchen, at some point you will want to melt some. It must be done with care because chocolate is an emulsion of cocoa butter: droplets of fat suspended in the cocoa solids. If the chocolate is heated up too much the cocoa butter droplets become very liquid and coalesce, and before you know it, the fat has completely separated, and the chocolate solids have clumped and turned grainy. Therefore, it is best to use caution and melt it in a bowl over just-simmering water. Chocolate buttons melt more quickly and are easier to use than big blocks, which have to be broken up prior to use. Use the best chocolate you can afford when baking. I am not a fan of high-fat so-called cooking chocolate, and if possible, choose one that has been produced ethically. The easiest thing to make is a ganache, that silky mixture of chocolate and cream, a wonderful substance which seems to have been devised very soon after Lindt produced his conche-ground chocolate bars. Here, cream is heated until scalding hot (but not boiling), then it's taken off the heat and the chocolate is beaten in with a small whisk. The magic ratio is two parts cream to one part chocolate, which makes a ganache that can be used as a sauce for profiteroles or poured into a blind-baked pastry case for a *tarte au chocolate*. A knob of butter gives a ganache a very pleasing glossiness. Ganaches can be whipped until cool to make a mousse-like product that is excellent for sandwiching chocolate cakes.

A whole array of decorations can be made from melted chocolate, and most are beyond my patience levels, though I have been known to paint a leaf with chocolate. Those who are inclined can brush it on curled acetate or scrape it into bows and cigarettes; but tackling these things is an aneurism waiting to happen if you ask me. Even if you are doing something as simple as a leaf or some squiggles on parchment paper, the effect can be somewhat dampened if the chocolate hasn't been tempered properly. Tempered chocolate has shine and snap. The process of mixing, heating and cooling isn't straightforward, but the clever Swiss worked it out very quickly. In the process of tempering, writes Sam Bilton in *The Philosophy of Chocolate* (2023), 'the temperature of the liquid chocolate is raised and lowered to avoid the formation of crystals in the solid chocolate, which can appear mottled and discoloured in a condition known as blooming'.[11] Different temperatures have to be hit with different types of chocolate, but with milk chocolate, for example, it must be melted to a temperature of 45 to 50 degrees Celsius, and then cooled to between 27 and 28 degrees. This can be achieved in two ways: the original marbling method, where the heated chocolate is poured on to a marble worktop, the outermost edges of the pool scraped into the centre until smooth and evenly cooled. The other method is better for those who don't have access to a marble worktop – i.e. most of us. Chocolate is melted to the correct temperature in a bowl, and then it is placed on a bowl of iced water. The downside of this method is that it can cool the chocolate too quickly. The first true chocolatiers did all of this by eye and feel; today we can use digital thermometers. The process certainly takes a little practice and patience, and the main issue really is that the process is difficult when using just a small amount of chocolate. Slow cooling is essential because it means small fat crystals and shiny chocolate with snap.

All of this said, I think that the best use for melted chocolate is to fold it into floppily whipped cream (with or without sugar), pour it into pots and let it set in the fridge to make a mousse. Decadence need not be an effort.

CHOCOLATE LOGS

The ancient tradition of the Yule log burning throughout the entire midwinter period in pre-Christian Europe has been attributed to the Celts, Vikings and Gauls, depending on where you read about it. We seem to get wrapped up in the romance of these ancient practices and treasure the links to these almost mythical people. The Yule log was, supposedly, a huge log that was kept burning throughout the Yuletide period. This custom is so old that we cannot be sure of the real origins, or how it was practised, and so many of the accounts of it date centuries after it supposedly occurred, usually written by Victorian gents who wanted a return to simpler Christmases. One has to take it all with a pinch of salt. Even more tenuous, then, is the chocolate Yule log, or *bûche de Noël*, having a similarly ancient origin. This is obviously nonsense, bearing in mind it is made up of a genoise chocolate Swiss roll, covered in ganache and filled with buttercream. Chocolate is a New World food, sugar wasn't brought to the British Isles in any significant amount until the thirteenth century, and rollable sponge cakes are a nineteenth-century invention.

It is a beautiful confection, though, when made well. One of the best recipes is Delia Smith's: a flourless chocolate Swiss roll filled with whipped cream and *crème de marrons* (purée of candied sweet chestnuts). Heaven. Then there are the beautiful decorations: the ganache bark, the sculpted leaves and mushrooms and perhaps some woodland creatures rendered in marzipan. Pastry chefs get very competitive about their beautiful, intricately decorated and often rather abstract interpretations of it. In recent years it has been ruined by mass-production – cheap, dry Swiss roll, brown in colour (though not chocolatey in taste), flavoured with fake vanilla essence. Most home-made *bûches de Noël* invariably begin with a shop-bought cake, I think because people are put off making a Swiss roll, expecting it to be too difficult. A proper Swiss roll is made with a genoise sponge mixture, so it's not a beginner's cake, but making a chocolate log is the best time to have a go at it; any cracks that appear can be covered with ganache, icing sugar snow or a host of sugar toadstools.

To make a Swiss roll, sponge mixture is poured into a lined, shallow Swiss roll tin and baked for just a few minutes. Once cooked, it's cooled on a rack in its tin for five minutes. A square of greaseproof paper just wider than the length of the tin is laid out. The cake is turned onto it, the lining is peeled away, and the sponge rolled up in the paper. When cold, it's ready to use. The delicate sponge will now be easy to roll, and who cares if there's the odd crack – it will taste better than any store-bought version.

CHARLOTTE RUSSE

Modern patisserie is exciting, bright and created with scientific precision, but high-class patisserie, desserts and confectionery would not be what they are today without the French chefs of the late-eighteenth and nineteenth centuries who were employed by royalty and gentry across Europe. They were given huge budgets, allowing their imaginations to run riot, coming up with techniques and inventions that would not have been economically viable in any patisserie, no matter how swish. Historian Peter Brears said of this cohort that their creations were of 'astounding artistic and technical magnificence'.[12] Of this group, Antoine Carême is the most famous, and his story is a very romantic one because he was born into a very large and very poor family, but such was his drive and skill that he clambered through the ranks to be the chef to several powerful people, including Tsar Alexander I of Russia, the Rothschilds and even the Bonapartes; politics were obviously not an issue for him. From the point of view of British baking, it is his tenure as the chef to Prince George, the Prince Regent and future George IV, infamous for his reckless spending and high living, that is of particular interest. Carême infamously hated English cuisine, and for him the worst were puddings: too stodgy, too plain and too simple. While working for the prince he decided to turn the simple apple Charlotte into a popular masterpiece. The original pudding is made by lining a mould with bread, filling it with stewed apple, covering the top with more bread, baking it and turning it out for serving. Carême made this humble affair fancy and extravagant by swapping the bread for boudoir biscuits and using them to line fancy copper moulds. Sometimes the biscuits on the bottom of the mould were replaced with candied fruits set in a clear, flavoured jelly. The mould was filled with a bavarois, a whipped cream mousse set with gelatine. Favourite flavours were chocolate, coffee or vanilla. He had named it *Charlotte parisienne*, but changed it to *russe*, the reason is not entirely clear, but it may have been changed in honour of a visiting Tsar Alexander I, or because it was a nod to the trendy new way of dining – service *à la russe*, or Russian service – where food was brought out in several, separate courses, which we continue to use today, of course; some fashions stick around.

Carême worked in several places before returning to France to write his cookery books. He is still revered today, but his approach has been subject to some reassessment. Yes, he was a genius, but one does not rise to the top on aptitude alone, and he 'used money, political power and social connections to enhance his reputation'.[13] He was as wasteful as he was pretentious, and historian Barbara Wheaton said of him that 'his exaggerated self-importance carried him further than modesty would have done'.[14]

Carême may have viewed British cuisine with contempt, but his protégé Charles Elmé Francatelli thought British cuisine, when cooked properly, was the best in the world, and he set about applying what he had learnt from his teacher to British foods. It is with him that we shall conclude our history of baking.

AFTERWORD:
BRING ME THE HEAD
OF CHARLES ELMÉ
FRANCATELLI

Most history books take us to the present day to make their conclusions, but not this one. Sure, we can make and decorate a cake that can appear to be something else. TV game shows have been made using them, asking contestants to guess 'Is it cake? Or is it a shoe?' or whatever. But we are stopping in the mid-nineteenth century, because I believe it is here that we reached the pinnacle of patisserie perfection, thanks to the good work of Charles Elmé Francatelli, who made fantastic *trompe-l'oeil* ('trick of the eye') creations without the aid of edible paint and mouldable, mass-produced fondant icing. This chap was the real deal. As a pupil of Carême's he was quickly snapped up as chef to Queen Victoria, but in addition to this, he loved British food – he was British and of Italian heritage – and Carême's snobbishness had not worn off on him in that regard. Instead, he applied what he had learned from the master and elevated British food, made it excellent again, revered once more. He was not without fault; he was rude and argumentative, and was even suspended from his position after creating, what we would call today, a toxic working environment.

Since at least the Middle Ages, *trompe-l'oeil* dishes have delighted diners: meatballs disguised as apples, or almond-milk jelly eggs were popular medieval table curiosities. Eighteenth-century confectioner Elizabeth Raffald took things further with her spectacular yet subtle cribbage cards and bacon and eggs made from jelly. Francatelli made an 'imitation Ham made of Savoy Biscuits and filled with Cream Ice'. Very cute. However, he also produced the showstopper to end all showstoppers, beating those made by cake decorators today hands down: his spectacular boar's head cake.

The real boar's head used to be the centrepiece of the Christmas sideboard, and it was quite a thing to behold: a boned, stuffed and poached pig's head presented piped over with lard blackened with charcoal, decorated in piped lard flowers, and glazed in aspic. It was then made splendid, adorned with silver spears upon which were impaled black truffles and poached cockscombs. It was finished with bunches of herbs plunged into its ears and mouth. There is a very hazy photograph of Queen Victoria's Christmas sideboard furnished with such delights as a baron of beef, a woodcock pie and a regal boar's head.

The details of Francatelli's confectionary creation are detailed in his 1862 book *The Royal and Foreign Confectioner* and it contains a very helpful colour lithograph illustration of it, which looks amazingly like the real thing. The number of techniques required to pull it off is remarkable, and that they are all done without modern electrical gadgets or refrigeration makes the feat all the more awesome.

To begin, five Savoy cakes were made from 1.5 kilograms of batter, which were cooled and glued together with apricot jam to form an approximate head shape, before being carved more precisely and painted over with melted redcurrant jelly. Next, the whole thing was glazed in a layer of shiny chocolate icing. Tusks and eyes were made from sugar paste, with eyes dipped in a molten sugar syrup (soft-crack stage, please) to give them a realistic, glassy appearance. Once fixed in place 'the mouth is to be hollowed out, and coloured of a deep scarlet inside with royal icing'. Silver skewers were then decorated with marzipan cockscombs, sugared fruits and chocolate truffles, before being plunged into the head at artistic angles.* Just before service 'the throat end is to be hollowed out to receive the ice, which must be frozen stiff, and of two colours in imitation of the flesh – pink and white – to give it the appearance of fat and lean in natural layers'.[1] The head was sat upon its stand (made from confectioner's paste – a mix of eggs, sugar and flour – and marzipan) and decorated all around with cubes of fruit jelly, to represent the usual aspic garnish.

It is a wonder of the pâtisserie world: so British, so playful, yet took a huge amount of skill and resources to produce. It was a feat in both planning and imagination. In short, a work of genius, and as far as I'm concerned, it's all downhill from here.

---

* Interestingly, historian Ivan Day believes this to be the first time chocolate truffles appear in a cookery book.

ACKNOWLEDGEMENTS

My sincere thanks to everyone whom I have spoken with regarding the intricacies of British baking, whether that be in person or as a contributor to *The British Food History Podcast*: Sam Bilton, Marc Meltonville, Elaine Lemm and Aaron Allen. Special thanks to Ivan Day for his expert tutelage and advice regarding historic pie making.

I am eternally grateful to my friends and family for their unwavering support, especially Hugh Roberts, who just might be the most patient person on the planet.

BIBLIOGRAPHY & REFERENCES

BOOKS

Acton, E. (1845) *Modern Cookery for Private Families*. Quadrille.

Acton, E. (1859) *The English Bread Book*. Edited by E. Ray. Southover Press.

Anon (1737) *The Whole Duty of a Woman*. 1st edn. London: T. Read.

Apicius, Grocock, C.W. and Grainger, S. (2006) *Apicius: A Critical Edition*. Edited by C.W. Grocock and S. Grainger. Prospect Books.

Austin, T. (ed.) (1888) *Two Fifteenth-Century Cookery Books*. The Early English Text Society.

Avery, V. and Calaresu, M. (2019) *Feast & Fast: The Art of Food in Europe, 1500–1800*. Bloomsbury USA.

Balinska, M. (2008) *The Bagel: The Surprising History of a Modest Bread*. Yale University Press.

Beckett, S.T. (2007) *The Science of Chocolate*. Royal Society of Chemistry.

Beeton, I. (1861) *The Book of Household Management*. Lightning Source.

Beeton, I. (1923) *Mrs. Beeton's Cookery Book*. Ward, Lock & Company.

Bilton, S. (2021) *First Catch Your Gingerbread*. Prospect Books.

Bilton, S. (2022) *Fool's Gold: A History of British Saffron*. Prospect Books.

Bilton, S. (2023) *The Philosophy of Chocolate*. British Library.

Boxer, A. (2012) *Arabella Boxer's Book of English Food*. Fig Tree.

Brears, P. (2012) *Cooking & Dining in Medieval England*. Prospect Books.

Brears, P. (2014) *Traditional Food in Yorkshire*. Prospect Books.

Brears, P. (2015) *Cooking & Dining in Tudor & Early Stuart England*. Prospect Books.

Brears, P. (2023) *Cooking & Dining in the Victorian Country House*. Prospect Books.

Brillat-Savarin, J.A. and Fisher, M.F.K. (1949) *The Physiology of Taste or Meditations on Transcendental Gastronomy*. Everyman's Library.

Bruce-Gardyne, L. and Spaull, S. (2016) *Leiths Techniques Bible*. Bloomsbury.

Buttery, N. (2022) *A Dark History of Sugar*. Pen & Sword History.

Buttery, N. (2023) *Before Mrs Beeton: Elizabeth Raffald, England's Most Influential Housekeeper*. Pen & Sword History.

Chambers, W. and Chambers, R. (eds) (1855) *Chambers's Edinburgh journal*. W. and R. Chambers.

David, E. (1977) *English Bread and Yeast Cookery*. Grub Street.

David, E. (1984) *An Omelette and a Glass of Wine*. The Lyons Press.

David, E. (2000) *Is There a Nutmeg in the House?* Edited by J. Norman. Penguin Books.

Davidson, A. (1999) *The Oxford Companion to Food*. Oxford University Press.

Dawson, T. (1596) *The Good Housewife's Jewel*. 1996 Edition. Southover Press.

DeRosa, R. (2009) *The Making of Salem: The Witch Trials in History, Fiction and Tourism*. McFarland.

Digby, K. (1669) *The Closet of Sir Kenelm Digby Opened* (1997 reprint). Edited by J. Stevenson and P. Davidson. Prospect Books.

Dillon, C.F. and Peterson, D.J. (2023) *A Cook's Perspective: A Fascinating Insight Into 18th-century Recipes by Two Historic Cooks*. Casemate.

DiMuzio, D.T. (2010) *Bread Baking: An Artisan's Perspective*. John Wiley & Sons.

Drummond, J.C. and Wilbraham, A. (1939) *The Englishman's Food: Five Centuries of English Diet*. Pimlico.

Estérelle Payany, A.J. (2017) *French Pâtisserie: Master Recipes and Techniques from the Ferrandi School of Culinary Arts*. Flammarion.

Farley, J. (1783) *The London Art of Cookery, and Housekeeper's Complete Assistant*. Price.

Farmer, F. (1979) *The Fannie Farmer Cookbook*. 12th edn. Edited by M. Cunningham and J. Laber. Bantam Books.

Farmer, F.M. (1896) *The Boston Cooking-school Cook Book*. 1st edn. Little, Brown.

Findlay, W.M. (1956) *Oats: Their cultivation and use from ancient times to the present day*. Oliver and Boyd Ltd.

Fintz, M. (2019) *The History of Bagels in America*. Lulu.com.

FitzGibbon, T. (1971) *A Taste of Wales*. London: J M Dent & Sons Ltd.

FitzGibbon, T. (1983) *Irish Traditional Food*. St. Martin's Press.

Francatelli, C.E. (1862) *The Royal English and Foreign Confectioner*. Chapman and Hall.

Francatelli, C.E. (1906) *The Modern Cook*. Macmillan and Co. Ltd.

Gellatly, J. (2016) *Bread, Cake, Doughnut, Pudding Sweet and Savoury Recipes from Britain's Best Baker*. Penguin Books Limited.

Glasse, H. (1747) *The Art of Cookery Made Plain and Easy*. Prospect Books.

Goldstein, D. (ed.) (2015) *The Oxford Companion to Sugar and Sweets*. Oxford University Press.

Gray, A. (2017) *The Greedy Queen: Eating with Victoria*. Profile.

Gray, A. (2021) *At Christmas We Feast: Festive Food Through the Ages*. Profile.

Grigson, J. (1969) *Charcuterie and French Pork Cookery*. Grub Street.

Grigson, J. (1982) *Jane Grigson's Fruit Book*. Penguin.

Grigson, J. (1992) *English Food*. Third Edit. Penguin.

Grivetti, L.E. and Shapiro, H.-Y. (2011) *Chocolate: History, Culture, and Heritage*. Wiley.

Hanneman, L.J. (2009) *Patisserie*. 2nd edn. Taylor & Francis.

Harrison, S. (1751) *The House-keeper's Pocket-book and Compleat Family Cook*. 5th edn. R. Ware.

Hartley, D. (1954) *Food in England*. Little, Brow.

Hartley, D. (1979) *Lost Country Life*. Macdonald & Janes.

Henisch, B. (2009) *The Medieval Cook*. Boydell.

Hieatt, C.B. and Butler, S. (1985) *Curye on Inglysch: English culinary manuscripts of the fourteenth century*. Oxford University Press.

Hollywood, P. (2013) *How to Bake*. Bloomsbury.

Hughes, G. (2016) *The Lost Feast of Christmas*. Lulu.com.

Hutchins, S. (1967) *English Recipes, and others from Scotland, Wales and Ireland as they appeared in eighteenth and nineteenth century cookery books and now devised for modern use*. Cookery Book Club.

James, A. (1996) 'Cooking the Books: Global or local identities in contemporary British food cultures?', in D. Howes (ed.) *Cross-cultural Consumption: Global Markets, Local Realities*. Routledge.

Katz, S.E. (2012) *The Art of Fermentation*. Chelsea Green.

Kay, E. (2023) *Fodder & Drincan: Anglo-Saxon Culinary History*. Prospect Books.

Larousse Gastronomique (2001). Hamlyn.

Lemm, E. (2018) *The Great Book of Yorkshire Pudding*. Great Northern Books Limited.

Markham, G. (1633) *Country Contentments, or The English Huswife*. J. Harison.

Markham, P. (1757) *Poison Detected*. Messrs.; Dodsley, Osbourne, Corbet, Griffith and James.

Mason, L. and Brown, C. (1999) *The Taste of Britain*. Devon: Harper Press.

May, R. (1685) *The Accomplisht Cook (1660/85)*. Edited by A. Davidson, M. Bell, and T. Jaine. Prospect Books.

McGee, H. (1984) *On Food and Cooking: The Science and Lore of the Kitchen*. 1st edn. Allen and Unwin.

McNeill, F.M. (1968) *The Scots Kitchen: Its Lore & Recipes*. 2nd edn. Blackie & Son Limited.

Miller, Emily Elyse (2019) *Breakfast: The Cookbook*. Phaidon Press.

Miller, M. and Volkwein, A. (2023) *Tasting History Explore the Past Through 4,000 Years of Recipes*. S&S/Simon Element.

Moffett, T. (1746) *Health's Improvement*. Edited by W. Oldys. T. Osbourne.

Parry, I. (2018) *The Evolution of Cornbread*, Medium.

Pepys, S. (1895) *The Diary of Samuel Pepys*. Edited by R. Griffin. G. Bell.

Purkiss, D. (2023) *English Food: A People's History*. William Collins.

Raffald, E. (1769) *The Experienced English Housekeeper*. First Edit. J. Harrop.

Randolph, M. (1836) *The Virginia Housewife: or, Methodical Cook*. John Plaskitt .

Report of the Missouri State Horticultural Society for the Year 1808 (1808). Tribune Printing Company.

Shanahan, M. (2019) *Christmas Food and Feasting: A History*. Rowman & Littlefield.

Smith, A.F. (2007) *The Oxford Companion to American Food and Drink*. Oxford University Press.

Smith, D. (1982) *Delia Smith's Complete Cookery Course*. BBC Books.

Snodgrass, M.E. (2004) *Encyclopedia of Kitchen History*. Taylor & Francis Group.

Soyer, A. (1855) *A Shilling Cookery for the People: Embracing an Entirely New System of Plain Cookery and Domestic Economy*. Routledge & Co.

Stevens, D. (2009) *River Cottage Handbook No.3: Bread*. Bloomsbury.

Sukhadwala, S. (2022) *The Philosophy of Curry*. British Library.

Toussaint-Samat, M. (1992) *History of Food*. Blackwells.

Vaughan, J.G. and Geissler, C.A. (2009) *The New Oxford Book of Food Plants*. 3rd Edition. Oxford University Press.

Vogler, P. (2023) *Stuffed: A History of Good Food and Hard Times in Britain*. Atlantic Books.

Wareing, M. and Wright, J. (2014) *How to Cook the Perfect ...* Dorling Kindersley Limited.

Wells, R. (2016) 'The Modern Practical Bread Baker', in *The Classic Guide to Breadmaking*. Amberley.

White, F. (1932) *Good Things in England*. Persephone.

Wilson, B. (2012) *Consider the Fork: A History of How We Cook and Eat*. Penguin Books Limited.

W.M. (1662) *The Compleat Cook*. Nath. Brooke.

de Worde, W. (1897) 'The Boke of Keruynge', in F.J. Furnivall (ed.) *Early English Meals and Manners*. The Early English Text Society.

Wrangham, R.W. (2010) *Catching Fire: How Cooking Made Us Human*. Profile Books.

Ysewijn, R. (2015) *Pride and Pudding: The History of British Puddings Savoury and Sweet*. Murdoch Books.

Zeide, A. (2023) *US History in 15 Foods*. Bloomsbury Academic.

JOURNALS AND NEWSPAPERS

'Accidental Explosions' (1875) *Nature*, pp. 478–479.

Bedford, C.C. (1896) 'Housekeepers' Inquiries', *Table Talk*, 11, pp. 121–121.

Burkette, A. (2011) '"Stamped Indian": Finding history and culture in terms for American "cornbread"', *American Speech*, 86(3).

Dalgetty, L. (2022) 'Remembering the Glasgow Flour Mill explosion that killed 18 people', *Glasgow Live*, 10 July.

Farah, T. (2019) *Banned bread: why does the US allow additives that Europe says are unsafe?*, *Guardian*.

Güldemir, O. (2022) 'Baklava Recipes from the Greek King Otto I to the Present', *Athens Journal of Mediterranean Studies*, 8(2).

Fuller Whiteman, E. (1938) *Miscellaneous Publication*. U.S. Department of Agriculture.

Kelsey, M.W. (1995) 'The Pudding Club and Traditional British Puddings', in H. Walker (ed.) *Disappearing Foods Studies in Foods and Dishes at Risk: Proceedings of the Oxford Symposium on Food and Cookery 1994*. Prospect Books.

Kennedy, P. (2012) *Who Made That Whisk?*, *The New York Times Magazine*.

Kindy, D. (2019) *For 100 Years, KitchenAid Has Been the Stand-Up Brand of Stand Mixers*, *Smithsonian Magazine*.

Lerch, S. (1979) 'A Feast of Blini', *The New York Times*, 28 February.

Manchester Guardian (1935) 'B.M.A.'s Suggestions for Cheap Meals', 6 September.

Mantle, P. (2020) 'Comparative ergot alkaloid elaboration by selected plectenchymatic mycelia of *Claviceps purpurea* through sequential cycles of axenic culture and plant parasitism', *Biology*, 9(3).

Michael, C. (2017) 'The Ambridge Paradox: Cake Consumption and Metabolic Health in a Defined Rural Population', in *Custard, Culverts and Cake: Academics on Life in The Archers*.

O'Connell, K. (2021) 'Breadlines and Banana Bread: Rethinking Our Relationship with Food in the Age of Covid-19', *Diplomatic History*.

Shewry, P. (2019) 'What is gluten—Why is it special?', *Frontiers in Nutrition*.

Wilson, C.A. (1985) 'I'll to Thee a Simnel Bring', *Petits Propos Culinaires*, 19, pp. 46–52.

BLOGS AND WEBSITES

Anon. (2022) 'Tea dunking test finds Hobnob-style does the perfect job', *BBC News*.

Austin, C.M. (2021) 'Lemon drizzle cake memories take me back to the 1950s', *Guardian Letters*.

Blakemore, E. (2017) 'The Delicious Democratic Symbolism of … Doughnuts?', *JSTOR Daily*.

Briggs, H. (2018) 'Prehistoric bake-off: Scientists discover oldest evidence of bread', *BBC News*.

Buttery, N. *British Food: A History*.

Buttery, N. *Neil Cooks Grigson*.

Cloake, F. (2021) 'How to make the perfect Sachertorte', *Guardian*.

Cocking, L. (2018) 'Why the UK has so many words for bread', *BBC Travel*.

Daley, J. (2017) 'Untouched, Century-Old Fruitcake Found in Antarctica', *Smithsonian*.

Day, I. *Food History Jottings*.

Dunning, A. (2017) 'The medieval origins of Mothering Sunday', *Medieval Manuscripts*.

Evins, A. 'Pastry Creams', *The Shortli.st*.

Franklin, L. and McNamee, G.L. 'focaccia', *Britannica*.com.

Geddes, K. (2013) 'It's All In The Booklet #2 – Petits Fours', *Keep Calm and Fanny On*.

Gibbons, B. (2021) 'Lemon Drizzle is UK's favourite cake – but size of slices should be bigger', *Wales Online*.

Gregory, J. (2023) *Pompeii archaeologists discover 'pizza' painting*, *BBC News*.

Hassani, N. (no date) 'Pumpernickel', *196 Flavours*.

HMRC *VFOOD6260* – 'Excepted items: Confectionery: The bounds of confectionery, sweets, chocolates, chocolate biscuits, cakes and biscuits: The borderline between cakes and biscuits', *GOV.UK*.

Housman, A. (2023) 'The Slightly Gross Way the Mississippi Mud Pie Got Its Name', *Food Republic*.

'How do people refer to the bread pictured here?' *Our Dialects*.

Hubbel, D. (2023) 'Red Velvet Cake's Journey to The Juneteenth Table', *Atlas Obscura*.

Hughes, G. *The Foods of England Project*.

Lam, C. (2023) 'Mirror Glaze Recipe', *The Spruce Eats*.

Loth, S. (2018) 'The truth about wholemeal bread', *Which?*

McNamee, G.L. and Blake, S. 'brioche', *Britannica.com*.

Nzinga, F. and Stevens-Truss, R. (2022) 'This Month in Black History – Juneteenth Culinary Traditions', *Kalamazoo College website.*

'Panettone gives Christmas cake a run for its money' (2012) *The Standard.*

Rummel, R. 'Financiers', *Atlas Obscura.*

Salter, H. 'Top 10 most popular cake recipes', *BBC Good Food.*

Siciliano-Rosen, L., 'Key Lime Pie', *Britannica.com.*

Smith, M. (2018) 'Cobs, buns, baps or barm cakes: what do people call bread rolls?', *YouGov.*

Taylor, A.-L. (2012) 'Why is bread Britain's most wasted food?', *BBC News.*

Thomas, R.B. (2002) 'Fannie didn't invent measures', *Deseret News*, 17 March.

Wood, Z. (2022) 'Taking it cheesy: can panettone's new flavours see off the Christmas cake?', *Guardian.*

NOTES

GRIDDLE CAKES AND PANCAKES

1. Brears (2014) p.107.
2. David (1977) p.407.
3. McNeill (1968) p.179.
4. These percentages have been calculated from data found in Vaughan & Geissler (2009) p.226.
5. Johnston (1824) p.215.
6. Grigson (1992) p.331.
7. Mason & Brown (1999) p.396.
8. Hartley (1954) p.620.
9. These metrications are not used in the original recipe, I have instead used Jane Grigson's interpretation of the recipe from her book *English Food* (1992) pp.338–9.
10. Davidson (1999) p.571.
11. Grigson (1992) p.338.
12. Lerch (1979) 'A Feast of Blini', *New York Times*.
13. Brears (2012) p.355.
14. Farmer (1979) p.xiv.
15. David (1977) p.432.

16. These quotes are from Elizabeth David's *English Bread and Yeast Cookery* (1977) pp.342–3 and 350–1.
17. McGee (1984) p.457.

BREAD

1. Moffatt (1746) p.333–4.
2. Acton (1859) p.97.
3. Markham (1633) p.250.
4. De Worde (1897) p.157.
5. Acton (1859) pp.68–9.
6. Wells (2016) pp.128–9.
7. Acton (1859) p.53.
8. Gregory (2023).
9. David, E. (2000) p.232.
10. *Ibid.* p.234.
11. Stevens (2009) p.86.
12. David (1977) p.286.
13. This quote appears in David (1977) p.285.
14. Grigson (1992) pp.303–4.
15. Chambers & Chambers (1855) p.293.
16. May (1685) p.239.
17. David (1977) p.315.
18. *Ibid.* p.365.
19. Davidson (1999) p.418.
20. Randolph (1836) p.141.
21. Markham (1757) pp.5–6.

22. *Ibid* pp.16–7.
23. Acton, p.37.
24. Cocking, L. (2018).
25. Acton (1847) p.556.
26. Soyer (1855) p.165.

BISCUITS AND CAKES

1. Raffald (1779) p.253.
2. McNeill (1968) p.200.
3. Gray (2017) p.291.
4. Glasse (1747) p.138.
5. McGee (1984) p.554.
6. Beeton (1861) p.856.
7. *Ibid.* p.857.
8. David (1977) pp.427,461.
9. Digby (1669) p.446.
10. O'Connell (2021) p.561.
11. Farmer (1976) p.684.
12. Raffald (1769) p.243.
13. Beeton (1861) p.873.
14. Day (2017) *The Smithsonian.*
15. Gray (2021) p.189.
16. Laura Mason writing in Davison (1999) p.724.
17. *Table Talk* Vol II 1896 'Housekeeper's Inquiries' p.121.
18. Bilton, S. (2022) pp.145–6.
19. Austin, *Guardian Letters* 4 July 2021.

20. Michael, C. (2017).
21. Hubbel (2023) *Atlas Obscura*.
22. See VFOOD6260 – 'Excepted items: Confectionery'.

PIES AND PUDDINGS

1. Davidson (1999) p.587.
2. Hieatt & Butler (1985) pp.134–5.
3. Dawson (1596) p.70.
4. Acton (1845) p.344.
5. Dawson (1596) p.71.
6. Beeton (1861) p.680.
7. Avery & Calaresu (2019) p.141.
8. May (1685) pp.234–5.
9. Francatelli (1908) p.385.
10. Glasse (1747) pp.139–40.
11. Day (2012) 'Eat the Entire Creation if you Dare …', *Food History Jottings*.
12. Hartley (1954) p.265.
13. Pepys (1895) p.75.
14. 'ARRR YOU MAD? Historian sparks uproar by claiming the pasty was NOT invented in Cornwall', *The Sun* 9 April 2020.
15. W.M. (1662) p.145.
16. *Two Fifteenth Century Cookery Books* (1880) p.98.
17. Ysewijn (2015) p.159.

18. Day (2013) 'Lattice Top Tarts and Their Precursors', *Food History Jottings.*

19. Beeton (1861) p.642.

20. Raffald (1769) p.238.

21. Mason & Brown (1999) pp.229–30.

22. *Ibid.* p.228.

23. W.M. (1658) p.109.

24. Ivan Day (2012) 'Some Early Bakewell Pudding Recipes', *Food History Jottings.*

25. Quote from Ivan Day (2012) 'Some Early Bakewell Pudding Recipes', *Food History Jottings.*

26. Ysewijn (2015) p.173.

27. Hutchins (1967) p.312.

28. Grigson (1982) p.40.

29. Laura Mason writing in Davidson (1999) p.230.

30. *Report of the Missouri State Horticultural Society for the Year 1808*, p.80.

31. Raffald (1769) p.232.

32. *Ibid.* pp.234–5.

33. Glasse (1747) p.69.

34. Brears (2014) p.189.

35. Grigson (1992) p.288.

36. Quote from James (1996) p.89.

37. Quote from Kelsey (1995) p.122.

38. Davidson (1999) p.644.

39. Hartley (1954) p.629.

40. Brears (2014) p.271.

PATISSERIE

1. Laura Mason writing in Davidson (1999) p.584.
2. Ferrandi (2017) p.5.
3. Bruce-Gardyne & Spaull (2016) p.526.
4. Grigson (1969) p.292.
5. Davidson (1999) p.107.
6. Brillat-Savarin (1949) pp.266–7.
7. David (1977) p.511.
8. Hanneman (2009) p.262.
9. Boxer (2012) p.204.
10. Beeton (1861) p.870.
11. Bilton (2023) p.103.
12. Brears (2023) p.156.
13. *Larousse Gastronomique* (2001) p.220.
14. Barbara Wheaton writing in Davidson (1999) p.138.

AFTERWORD

1. Francatelli (1862) p.293.